T0328601

Cambridge Elements ≡

Elements in Ancient Egypt in Context
edited by
Gianluca Miniaci
University of Pisa
Juan Carlos Moreno García
CNRS Paris
Anna Stevens
University of Cambridge and Monash University

TECHNOLOGY AND CULTURE IN PHARAONIC EGYPT

Actor–Network Theory and the Archaeology of Things and People

Martin Fitzenreiter
Independent Researcher

CAMBRIDGE
UNIVERSITY PRESS

CAMBRIDGE
UNIVERSITY PRESS

Shaftesbury Road, Cambridge CB2 8EA, United Kingdom

One Liberty Plaza, 20th Floor, New York, NY 10006, USA

477 Williamstown Road, Port Melbourne, VIC 3207, Australia

314–321, 3rd Floor, Plot 3, Splendor Forum, Jasola District Centre, New Delhi – 110025, India

103 Penang Road, #05–06/07, Visioncrest Commercial, Singapore 238467

Cambridge University Press is part of Cambridge University Press & Assessment, a department of the University of Cambridge.

We share the University's mission to contribute to society through the pursuit of education, learning and research at the highest international levels of excellence.

www.cambridge.org
Information on this title: www.cambridge.org/9781009074353

DOI: 10.1017/9781009070300

First published 2023

A catalogue record for this publication is available from the British Library.

ISBN 978-1-009-07435-3 Paperback
ISSN 2516-4813 (online)
ISSN 2516-4805 (print)

Technology and Culture in Pharaonic Egypt

Actor–Network Theory and the Archaeology of Things and People

Elements in Ancient Egypt in Context

DOI: 10.1017/9781009070300
First published online: March 2023

Martin Fitzenreiter
Independent Researcher
Author for correspondence: Martin Fitzenreiter, post@m-fitzenreiter.de

Abstract: The inherent paradox of Egyptology is that the objective of its study – people living in Egypt in Pharaonic times – are never the direct object of its studies. Egyptology, as well as archaeology in general, approaches ancient lives through material (and sometimes immaterial) remains. This Element explores how, through the interplay of things and people – of non-human actants and human actors – Pharaonic material culture is shaped. In turn, it asks how, through this interplay, Pharaonic culture as an epistemic entity is created: an epistemic entity which conserves and transmits even the lives and deaths of ancient people. Drawing upon aspects of Actor–Network Theory, this Element introduces an approach to see technique as the interaction of people and things, and technology as the reflection of these networks of entanglement.

Keywords: agency, Actor–Network Theory, technology, episteme, ancient Egypt

ISBNs: 9781009074353 (PB), 9781009070300 (OC)
ISSNs: 2516-4813 (online), 2516-4805 (print)

Contents

1 Introduction: A Conceptual Framework

Descriptions of the technologies of ancient cultures often present a history of inventions and innovations in the field of technical procedures, including the development of tools (and weapons). Recent scholarship is enlarging this focus from the description of techniques and tools towards the circumstances driving technical change. Additionally, interactions between people and their wider environments are gaining attention in the field of technological studies.[1] This Element aims to provide a theory-centred discussion on topics and terminology within the study of ancient techniques, as well as on research on technological reflection in antiquity. The approach is illustrated by examples from the Egyptological expertise of the author. Each section starts with an introduction to a number of key conceptual approaches and their sometimes complicated terminologies, followed by a case study which roots these approaches in archaeological reality. Since the Element is not intended to be a technological handbook or a history of techniques, readers will have to refer to the references for details on specific methods of production.[2] The same holds true for the terminological side, since for the sake of succinctness, epistemic foundations are sometimes presented only quite briefly.[3]

1.1 Things As Actants

The topic of this Element is an archaeology of the interplays between things and people and how they are 'assembled'. Interestingly, this conjuncture is inherent to the root of the word 'thing', the meaning of which in various Germanic languages evolved via 'date (to assemble)' through to 'assembly' and 'matter (that assembles)', up to the current term for '(material) thing' or 'object' (Pfeifer, 2011: 227; Hodder, 2012: 8). According to Actor–Network Theory (ANT), things are what 'assemble' people: objects in action or actants, that is, entities, urging actors to (re)act (Latour, 2005). A *thing* is an *object* at interplay. It is thus on the non-human side. The counterparts on the human side are *people* and the *human body*: people are acting/interplaying human bodies (Turner, 2012). Putting things in relation to humans in this way, ANT provides a metatheory of human/non-human interplay that is quite useful for archaeology, but with a certain twist. Sociology – of which ANT is a branch – studies

---

[1] For the wider environment (*Umwelt*) in relation to systems (social or non-social) in the sense of system or networktheory see: Luhmann, 1987: 36–7.

[2] The most comprehensive handbook on Pharaonic technology remains Shaw & Nicholson, 2000. See also the approach to technology as a social phenomenon presented in Shaw, 2012 and in Müller-Wollermann, 2021. Readers are advised to consult these studies for further insight.

[3] Sections 1, 4 and 5 summarise topics discussed in some detail in Fitzenreiter, 2020, while Sections 2, 3 and 6 deal with additional aspects.

the human/non-human interplay exactly that way round: how humans are affected by things and how networks of human actors (people), as well as of non-human actants (things), interplay. Archaeology, intriguingly, acts the other way round: people's lives and deaths and everything around are the objective of archaeology, but they are not the immediate objects of its studies. Rather, these objects are material remains, even human remains, and any other evidence in space and time. Archaeology, seen as to "infer human behaviour and ideas from the material remains of what human beings have made and used and their physical impact on the environment" (Trigger, 1989: 19), is the science of the interplay of things and people. Exactly this way round.

1.2 Technique As Interaction

To grasp the difference between technique and technology is not always easy. Technique – at least in its German writing *Technik* – may be just used as a synonym for a body of technical devices. Nevertheless, it mostly describes a certain way of doing. There are techniques of cultivating plants, of cooking, of making pottery, of healing, of writing. In the following discussion, the term technique is used to designate any (conscious) interaction of humans with an Other. Interaction with objects is, of course, what the everyday use of the word implies, as, for example, with techniques of cooking, writing, and so on. But there are variants, as with techniques of persuasion and the like, which lead to a more complex concept of entities to interact with. As well as biotic or abiotic – human and non-human – objects, entities to interact with may also be phenomena such as wind, heat, and wetness. There are spiritual entities such as demons and gods. And there are simply ideas, such as health, fortune, and destiny. Sometimes these entities include even the self (Marcus Aurelius Antoninus, 1992). All of these manifestations of the Other are substantialised differently, and their *materiality* need not only be a material composition, but could be any other element of which it is constituted, be it stone or sound, silt or smell, script or thought (Kalthoff, Cress, & Röhl, 2016).

Interaction with these phenomena in the technical sense is in most cases conscious interaction, because it is constituted of two components: of manipulation and communication. Manipulation is the doing itself, that is, volitional interference in any kind of materiality. Communication means the exchange of information during the process of interfering. In the case of a craft, this may be information on the peculiarities of the specific material one is dealing with. In other cases, it is learning about feelings, ideas, and gods. Sharing that information is not just transmission, but is at the same moment a form of technical manipulation (or processing). It implies the creation of knowledge. Even if not regarded as the main task of the operation in most cases, but rather a by-product of handling, there is always a body of knowledge – a lasting experience – that is produced, not only in the mind of people but also in the Other that one is interacting with. Every interaction leaves an imprint: a piece of information.

1.3 Technology As Appropriation

As with technique, technology may be understood in different ways. If a certain set of techniques is combined in one or more steps of a *chaîne opératoire* (operational sequence), one may speak of a process or a technology. Lost-wax casting, often labelled as either the lost-wax casting process or lost-wax casting technology, provides an example. This Element, however, very deliberately uses the term technology – stressing the element *logos* – to refer to the cognitive aspect of practice. Technology is the appropriation of technical interaction. Technology is experience and knowledge, produced by conscious interaction between humans and other entities.

In contrast to techniques, technology may be studied in the archaeological record. Technique is pure practice; it has to be done. It is impossible to hand it over, to store it, to record it. What is handed over or stored is the knowledge of practice and the knowledge needed to practise. The latter may be just the impression of fingerprints in the fabric of a pot, recording knowledge of how to interact with clay, either by hand-building or throwing on a potter's wheel. It may also be a detailed description in a medical papyrus of how to produce a remedy. Thus, what remains and may be studied in archaeology are souvenirs of technical interaction stored in the memory of things.

'Memory of things' is an expression which should remind us that knowledge (= stored experience) is not confined to humans. The exchange of knowledge is bidirectional, affecting both the human and non-human side of interactions. It is important for archaeology to realise that it is not extracting human knowledge, but what has been stored as knowledge in and by objects, that is, to learn to extract the knowledge of things.[4] Technology is knowledge (of humans and non-humans) of technique.

1.4 Evidence As Media

To study evidence under this premise means to use it as a medium, transmitting information on the human past. More precisely: it means to use evidence as a medium of elements of knowledge, exchanged during technical interaction of this very evidence with people in the past. Knowledge thus stored in the

---

[4] For an ontology of things – what they really *are* beyond anthropocentric ontologies – see Harman, 2018.

evidence may then be transferred anew, as archaeologists entangle with the object in the present. Again, there is the important caveat: what archaeology is extracting is not knowledge of humans, but knowledge (determined/recorded/ processed) of things. The exchange of information with a given piece of evidence, once during a technical interaction and now during interaction by techniques of archaeological research, is both enabled as well as limited by medial capacities that the evidence possesses. Each object or entity reacts differently to human interference. A pot records aspects of its material composition, of processing, of handling, and maybe also of contents stored in it, among others. A papyrus records its materiality, production, and use, but, due to the script recorded on it, possesses other medial capacities as well, such as scribal techniques, a text, and even a message.

Paying attention to the bidirectional effects of interaction, we further have to consider that on the one side human interference – its intent and perception – affects the evidence, while on the other the evidence itself affects the process. The nature of the medium is part and parcel of the message. Media are not bare containers of knowledge, but processors (Winkler, 2015). A pictorial description of pottery on the walls of a funerary chapel mediates differently than a text, and so reports differently than a pot. The medial specificities of each kind of evidence need to be studied as their own branch of technology. Archaeology, to quite a considerable degree, is media capacity.

2 Technology and Archaeological Practice: Medicine

2.1 Research on Ancient Egyptian Techniques and Technology

Although we have to bear in mind that many techniques which are rooted in Pharaonic culture have never fallen into disuse or been forgotten in the Nile Valley, the following remarks are confined to what is generally called Egyptological studies, that is, research conducted by predominately western scholars after the forceful opening of Egypt to western exploitation and scholarship by the French military invasion in 1798, and the 1822 decipherment of the hieroglyphic script by Jean François Champollion. Besides studies on language, history, and religion, one objective of early Egyptological research was to collect and to describe the material conditions of Pharaonic culture. Outstanding among those early works is *The Manners and Customs of the Ancient Egyptians* by John Gardner Wilkinson (1837), a comprehensive *Kulturgeschichte* of Pharaonic Egypt. This work includes descriptions of techniques used in Pharaonic times as they may be studied from objects and depictions on the walls of tombs and temples (Figure 1). The book has what might be considered a companion volume in the similarly titled *Account of the*

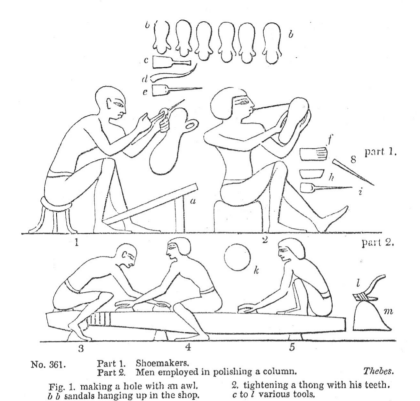

16Ω.   THE ANCIENT EGYPTIANS.   CHAP. IX.

No. 361.   Part 1. Shoemakers.
             Part 2. Men employed in polishing a column.   *Thebes.*

Fig. 1. making a hole with an awl.   2. tightening a thong with his teeth.
b b sandals hanging up in the shop.   *c* to *l* various tools.

Figure 1 'Shoemakers / Men employed in polishing a column'.
Source: illustration from Wilkinson (1837: 60), drawn after a depiction in a funerary chapel at Thebes.

Manners and Customs of the Modern Egyptians by Edward Lane (1890; written 1833–5). This volume presents a collection of data that paved the way for ethnoarchaeological comparisons even before the term ethnoarchaeology had been coined.

Approaches established by these early investigations, combining the vast amount of information in Pharaonic visual and written culture with observations of modern or early modern practice, form an important body of research in technical and technological topics up to the present day. Seminal studies – for example, on bread and beer preparation (Faltings, 1998), ceramic production (Holthoer, 1977; Arnold & Bourriau, 1993; Nicholson & Doherty, 2016), metalwork (Scheel, 1985, 1986, 1987), and water management and agriculture (Bonneau, 1964; Schenkel, 1978; Endesfelder, 1979) – are based, partly or completely, on the comparison of Pharaonic pictorial and written sources with material remains and ethnographic data.

Following a generation of collecting surface and near-to-surface materials, a new chapter of research opened in the last decades of the nineteenth century through systematically conducted excavations, with a focus not confined to inscriptions and 'beautiful objects' (Moreno Garcia, 2015: 52), but directed to the archaeological context. Pioneering in this respect were the archaeological endeavours of William M. Flinders Petrie and his team of trained excavators and qualified local workforce (Petrie, 1892: 156–66; Quirke, 2010; Doyon, 2015). Petrie's goal of establishing an encyclopaedic inventory of Pharaonic cultural expressions led to a series of studies on object groups and technical aspects of ancient Egyptian *Arts & Crafts* (Petrie, 1910). Those that figure most prominently are a number of catalogues from his collections at University College London, for example, *Amulets* (1914), *Tools and Weapons* (1917a), *Scarabs and Cylinders* (1917b) and *Objects of Daily Use* (1927). These volumes set a standard for similar corpus works and in-depth studies of object classes that form a substantial proportion of Egyptological literature; for example, on metal objects (Roeder, 1956; Weiss, 2012; Odler & Kmošek, 2020), textiles (Vogelsang-Eastwood, 1993), basketry (Wendrich, 1999), leatherwork (Veldmeijer, 2019), chariots (Veldmeijer & Ikram, 2013), woodwork (Killen, 2017), and so on.

The enormous increase in material resulting from fieldwork in turn led to new approaches to the study of material and technical properties, induced by the needs of conservation. With thousands of objects entering collections, methods for the safekeeping of artefacts had to be developed. Practitioners trained in chemistry began engaging with the field of antiquarian scholarship in the early twentieth century (Nicholson, 2010). Bridging the gap between humanities and sciences, their efforts led to the establishment of the field of archaeometry (Maggetti, 2006). In Egyptological research, one particularly prominent figure was Alfred Lucas, Chemist to the Antiquities Service of Egypt and author of the long-standing *Ancient Egyptian Materials and Industries* (1926). This hand-book has been updated four times (last edition revised by J. R. Harris in 1962) and only recently replaced by a work of similar character edited by Ian Shaw and Paul Nicholson, *Ancient Egyptian Materials and Technology* (2000). These, and quite a number of other publications, summarise results of research on the materiality of objects from Pharaonic Egypt conducted by conservators and scientists in archaeometry, for example, on faience (Kaczmarczyk, 1983), metal (Feisal, 1995; Eckmann & Shafik, 2002), papyrus (Graf & Krutzsch, 2008), and colour and painting (Dawson, Rozeik, & Wright, 2010), as well as on geomorphological and hydrological phenomena (Butzer, 1976). Due to the elaborate treatment of dead bodies in Pharaonic times, a special branch of research is constituted by the study of human and animal remains (David, 1986; Davies & Walker, 1993; Ikram, Kaiser, & Walker, 2015).

From around the 1970s, shifts towards long-term and large-scale studies of sites and heritage development have been accompanied by yet another turn in the recording and interpretation of material objects, adding the contextualising dimensions of time and space. Increasingly, archaeological projects are developing holistic approaches in order to create complex documentation of the archaeological matrix (Sigl, Kopp, & Fritzsch, 2018). Analysis of the multidimensional properties of evidence – including spatial position, context, materiality, and incorporated 'biography' – is a growing priority (Pusch & Rehren, 2007; Kemp & Stevens, 2010; Prell, 2011; Zakrzewski, Shortland, & Rowland, 2016). Connected to this, investigations of working spaces, reconstructions of the *chaîne opératoire*, of human–thing relationships, and of actor–networks, are on the agenda (Bader & Ownby, 2013; Moreno García, 2016; Steel & Zinn, 2017; Miniaci et al., 2018; Becker, Jungfleisch, & von Rüden, 2018; Hodgkinson & Tvetmarken, 2020; Bader, 2021a).

2.2 Research and Paradigm

As this brief overview demonstrates, each of these four archetypical modalities of engagement with Pharaonic technical and technological matter is not one piece of a successive pattern of development, but part of a historical matrix of archaeological research. At the same time, each of these methodological patterns is framed by wider contemporaneous approaches and attitudes to technical phenomena. Rooted in the age of industrial revolution, for example, works such as Wilkinson's and Lane's *Manners and Customs* are not only descriptions of traditional craft's past (and present) but also reflect the romantic rejection of industrialisation. Mirroring the Arts and Crafts movement (Morris et al., 1893), investigations into 'traditional' handicrafts and 'manners' of manufacture were inspired by a focus on techniques which was embedded in an anti-modernist attitude. Traditionalism, as well as Orientalism, have both been driven by the desire to find (and invent) an imagined stable timescape that is not railroaded forward by modernity (Moreno García, 2015). Description and reconstruction of ancient methods of production have also often been conducted not only as a goal in themselves, but for use as a source of inspiration. This holds true for a wider public, for whom Pharaonic patterns of design and style are adapted in any range of artisanal Egyptomania (Humbert, 1989). At the same time, this approach interplays with the outwardly scientific question of 'how the ancients did it', or experimental archaeology (Stocks, 2003; Graves-Brown & Goodridge, 2015; Rademakers et al., 2021). Whatever scientific information is pursued in an archaeological experiment, personal involvement in the process is a not unattractive side effect which helps to provide a vision of the skills required as well as deeper comprehension of the process (Gailhard, 2018). Direct involvement in the production process is at the roots of an 'archaeology of skill' (Wendrich, 2006; Kuijpers, 2018; Miniaci, 2021). Enactments and 'living-history' scenes take an even deeper step towards immersion into technical matters, where to use the right techniques testifies to a level of entanglement with the past, which is an intrinsic goal in itself (Willner, Koch, & Samida, 2016).

Being in a way the dialectic counterpart to this, approaches of classificatory archaeology developed in the late nineteenth century are deeply embedded in an evolutionary worldview that praises modernity and the structuring effect of railway time (Trigger, 1989: 148–206). Painting a picture not only of contingent *history* and its ephemere *events*, but of compelling *culture* and its inevitable *development*, classificatory archaeology models stages of evolution for all phenomena of society, religion, and material culture. Cultural units and their positions relative to others are defined and fixed in time and space via the classification of objects. Among the most classic outcomes of this approach are the typologies of ceramics, which in turn form the backbone of more or less any other typological effort (Petrie, 1901: 4–12; Bourriau, 2007). Once brought into a typological frame, typ(olog)ical objects, their typ(olog)ical production, and their typ(olog)ical use define cultural stages: stone age, bronze age, and so on. Within this scheme, in order to jump from one stage into the other, innovations are necessary: from technical achievements such as pottery, metallurgy, and seafaring; via increasingly differentiated types of social organisation such as tribe, chiefdom, and kingdom; up to religious progress from animism to monotheism. A legacy of this evolutionary approach is the central position of the concept of innovation or 'for the first time' in the study of the interplay of people and things: when and where a certain technical intervention is to be detected for the first time and how knowledge of it has spread in time and space (Shortland, 2001; Bourriau & Phillips, 2004; Mathieu, Meeks, & Wissa, 2006; Wilde, 2011; Shaw, 2017).

Both approaches – focussing on involvement in a craft and focussing on innovation – are at the heart of histories of techniques proper, that is, the history of how people shape and change their environment through tools and invention (Hessler, 2012). With an increasing interest in the properties of materials themselves, inspired by the fields of science and conservation, the other side of the interaction between people and things attracted a wider interest. Next to the wants of people, the wants of things moved into focus: what do cereals need to become a diet (Hayden, Nixon-Darcus, & Ansell, 2017), what makes mud a clay (Bourriau, Nicholson, & Rose, 2000: 121–7), and how and where are minerals to be mined (Pfeiffer, 2012)? Needs and networks of materials started to inspire the agenda of archaeometric investigation. It began to be recognised that it is not only people and their capacity to craft and invent that underlie technical mastery and innovation but also things and their properties, from their material peculiarities through to their availability in place and time. The concept of the *chaîne opératoire* most directly models this necessary interplay (Leroi-Gourhan, 1992): each step of production, use, re-use, and, finally, deposition of an object is directed not by human will (alone), but by the *Eigensinn* of things as well, leading to their 'life-use' or 'biography' (Hahn, 2015).

In the first half of the twentieth century, and independently of archaeometry, interest in this kind of entanglement of people and things also germinated among historians of sciences, stimulated by an interest in innovation and how it comes into being – or not. It appeared that *knowledge* plays a central role in the interplay of people and things and in how knowledge is shaped, shared, and circulated. Aristotelian approaches to this problem were initially widespread, and characterised by a strict distinction between techniques (*techné* / τέχνη) – the basic doing of things – and knowledge (*epistémé* / ἐπιστήμη) – that is, reflection on the reasons for why things are as they are (Blumenberg, 2009). Whereas the first is rated just a skill, the latter is prized as technological knowledge and the only requirement for innovation. This dichotomic view was foiled when research on the history of science revealed that the nature of things has been differently interpreted at different times – but unexpectedly there was still technical innovation, obviously on the basis of 'false' knowledge. Ludwik Fleck (1935) was among the first to bring this insight into a model of historical reception: knowledge is bound to the circumstances of its formation, and each time develops its own collectively shared explicatory style or framework of interpretation (*Denkstil* of a *Denkkollektiv*). Examples of this phenomenon are chemistry and astronomy, which each present ample bodies of evidence of explicatory frameworks or paradigms of scientific research. Thomas Kuhn (1970) showed how scientific explanation may stagnate because it remains within the borders of a given scientific paradigm, while techniques are exercised and practical knowledge accumulates in a manner that can far outgrow contemporaneous epistemological frameworks. In the second half of the twentieth century, sociologists and historians established the field of science and technology studies (STS) in order to explore how technical progress and knowledge are interwoven (Beck, Niewöhner, & Sørensen, 2012). The field of sociology, in particular, developed powerful counternarratives to the still predominant anthropocentric and evolutional approaches, by fathoming the roles things play in the interaction of humans and their environment. These approaches are summarised under the umbrella of Actor–Network Theory (ANT), which in a sense turns the axioms of causality upside down: it is not by people that society (or, more generally, the social) exists, but there are diffuse networks of different actors – human and non-human – shaping the social environment (Latour, 2005). Whatever concrete methodology has emerged from these approaches, there is little doubt that the shift to holistic archaeology, and also in the field of Egyptology, is rooted in this paradigmatic frame (Meskell, 2004), as well as the emerging interest in the properties of less tangible 'things', such as light(ning) (Strong, 2021) and smell (Goldsmith, 2022).

2.3 Case Study: Curing and Healing

An example of how research into ancient technology is shaped by such over-lapping premises is given by the history of medicine. The history of Pharaonic medicine in itself is a field with some peculiarities compared to other aspects of Pharaonic technology. Next to building techniques – especially pyramid construction – Egyptian medicine is probably the field with the highest rate of contributions by non-Egyptological professionals trained in other disciplines: in this case, in curative sciences.[5] Thus, research in medicine is tightly connected to approaches from outside Egyptology proper and makes for an interesting example of the interplay of historical research, modern science, and public attention. Research on Egyptian medicine is also of interest to a study on technology since medicine, like mathematics or astronomy, is normally not graded a technique but a science. Nevertheless, since medicine is the combination of specific practices, using specialised tools (instruments) and resources (drugs) on the one hand, and reflection on those practices, tools, and resources on the other, it should be included in general reflections on technological approaches, as the discipline of science and technology studies demonstrates (Knopes, 2019). To see Pharaonic medical practices as fundamentally different from technologies of, say, baking and pot making, is also to enable biases in Egyptological scholarship itself. Medical evidence includes a number of written resources which are generally prized as the media of knowledge par excellence in historical research. Besides, physicians are learned people with whom historians prefer to communicate, rather than engage with bakers and potters.

---

[5] See the extensive list of publications on Pharaonic medicine, many of them written by or in collaboration with medical practitioners, on: https://sae.saw-leipzig.de/de/literatur (accessed 17 April2021).

Evidence and the social customs of academia have thus shaped a certain 'style of thought' among scholars which led, right from the start, to a separation of medical from other humbler techniques.

In early research, using a melange of evolutionary interpretation and adopting paradigms from contemporary medicine, it became a kind of noble task to establish Pharaonic medicine as a precursor to contemporary clinical medicine. The purpose of such monumental collections of data as the nine-volume *Grundriss der Medizin der alten Ägypter* by Hermann Grapow, Hildegard von Deines, and Wolfhard Westendorf (1954–73) was to identify all the evidence, according to contemporary medical axioms, and to use this to define the progressive and innovative aspects of Pharaonic medicine (Figure 2). At the same time,

Figure 2 Medical treatment: surgical papyrus Edwin Smith (New York Academy of Medicine), recto col. 6 + 7, cases 12 to 20. Written around 1600 BCE, the text describes anatomical observations and the examination, diagnosis, treatment, and prognosis of forty-eight types of medical problems. Traumas are categorised either as 'an ailment which I will treat', 'an ailment with which I will contend', or 'an ailment not to be treated'. Although most of the text is written in a factual style, the verso contains some magical spells.

Source: Photograph by Jeff Dahl, public domain, via Wikimedia Commons; https://commons.wikimedia.org/wiki/File:Edwin_Smith_Papyrus_v2.jpg.

outlying elements could be separated and classified as 'magic'. Next, bio-scientific analyses of medical practices and chemical analyses of drugs explored what types of curative techniques and pharmaceuticals were 'already' known in Pharaonic times (Dawson, 1953; Cockitt & David, 2010). This approach combined a classificatory taming of evidence, its placement into a historical framework in which medicine was a steadily developing natural science, and the scientific analysis of material remains. It made possible a comprehensive view of ancient Egyptian medicine set within the frame of a modern medical paradigm, and thus reachable also for a wider non-Egyptological audience (Nunn, 1996; Westendorf, 1999; Strouhal, Vachala, & Vymazalová, 2014 / 2021).

Despite this predominantly clinical approach, 'magical' aspects of Pharaonic medical practices nevertheless aroused interest, as did in turn the 'style of thought' of Pharaonic healers (and patients) themselves. Paul Ghalioungui discussed the interplay of medical treatment and magical therapy in his classic *Magic and Medical Science in Ancient Egypt* (Ghalioungui, 1963, Arabic original 1960), which has been followed by a growing number of publications in more recent times (Walker, 1990; Karenberg & Leitz, 2002), including views on 'alternative' medicine (Baligh, 2010). All develop from an interest in non-clinical healing practices or, as it might be styled, the Arts and Crafts of TPM (traditional Pharaonic medicine).

Research on the magical components of therapy further profited from studies by Michel Foucault (1963) and others on the social construction of the body, the historicity of concepts of norm and deviation, and how divergences would be regulated (Turner, 2012). Thus, a new interest arose around the interplay of medication and cognition, or of curative practices and how they are reflected upon. This again led beyond the dichotomy of science versus magic and opened new ways to see Pharaonic medicine as an actor–network, including not only the healer and those to be healed but also social forces, demons, spirits, and so on (Fischer-Elfert, 2005) (Figure 3). Today, research on Pharaonic medicine has equal standing with approaches of STS, looking for the interplay of concept and practice of healing in contemporary contexts, as well with the (in)famous provocation of Bruno Latour, that Ramesses II could not have died of tuberculosis since tuberculosis was a discovery/invention of clinical medicine of the nineteenth century (Latour, 2000). The paradigmatic shift from an evolutionary perspective of self-developing medical progress to the complexity of the epistemic web spawning around Pharaonic sources on healing is at ease with recent trends in life sciences towards exploring the importance of what is defined as illness and what is defined as health, in order to explain the healing process – and in order to believe in it. A healer who is not convinced by their concept of healing and their methods cannot heal, and a patient is not able to recover if they

Figure 3 Magical healing: Horus Cippus, c. 360–343 BCE (Metternich stela;
New York, Metropolitan Museum of Art 50.85); a collection of magical
depictions and texts to cure poisoning by snakes and other animals. In order to
cure, water has to be poured over the object and drunk by the patient while spells
and magical stories are recited, such as the one of Isis healing her child Horus,
who was stung by a scorpion.
Source: photograph from www.metmuseum.org/art/collection/search/546037.

do not believe in the healing process. Both have to share a common 'style of
thought'. To explore its framework of ideas opens the way to an emic approach
to therapeutical techniques (Pommerening, 2017).

2.4 Paradigms Past and Present

The way ancient Egyptian healing methods have been analysed by modern research is in line with approaches to the histories of sciences such as mathematics and astronomy, as well as technologies in building, the processing of substances, and so on. In a way, it is a characteristic of any research into historic knowledge to oscillate within two hermeneutic circles. One of these circles is rooted in a specific world-view of modern western scholarship, shaping the goals and boundaries of research: for example, that medicine is not a craft but a science and that scientific progress is characterised by innovation, leading to the elimination of erratic or magical concepts. The other circle is constituted by the evidence and what it conserves of paradigms of the past. Research on ancient Egyptian medicine has to navigate both circles in order to meet a contemporary audience, their interests, and tasks. Scholars of medical history are often trained in Egyptology as well as in contemporary medical sciences, making it possible to address a contemporary – academic and medical – community of thought (Radestock, 2015). Beyond this accepted paradigmatic frame, historical research is often dismissed as esoteric and thus disqualified in academia.[6] Yet archaeological research has to surpass prevailing paradigms to be able to interpret the tight interplay of curation and cognition within a historic framework in which diseases are conceptualised as demons. To achieve this balance between *emic* and *etic*, recent Egyptological activities in medical studies are developing interesting platform projects, providing data for Egyptological as well as for non-Egyptological communities.[7]

3 Technology and Material Culture: Nutrition

3.1 Technique, Culture, and Archaeology

3.1.1 Technique

Technique is human–thing interaction. Because interaction leaves traces, these traces constitute what may be called material culture: the results of human actions. Interaction is, of course, not a phenomenon specific only to humans. Substances themselves interact, as do non-human beings (plants, animals): being is metabolism. Most interaction creates changes in material consistency, thus transforming an aspect of materiality, which can be understood as the specific being of an entity, both in consistency and form, as well as in time and space. As soon as interaction

---

[6] This occurs in what may be characterised simply as the drift to a different paradigmatic frame (Hornung, 1999).

[7] See the project 'Science in Ancient Egypt' of the *Sächsische Akademie der Wissenschaften zu Leipzig*: (https://sae.saw-leipzig.de/de) and the DFG-Graduiertenkolleg 1867 at the University of Maience "Frühe Konzepte von Mensch und Natur" (www.grk-konzepte-mensch-natur.uni-mainz.de/) (accessed 23 April 2021).

creates changes to materiality, it leaves traces within objects, bodies, concepts, and also in the archaeological record. Transformation is therefore at the heart of any technique. Changes themselves occur not only through external intervention, but are also controlled by materiality itself. As soon as its biotic metabolism is interrupted, for example, organic matter sets in motion processes of material transformation, such as drying or decay. Technical interaction makes use of such inherent potential for transformation, for example, the increase in cell stability in dried wood or the splitting of nutrients via controlled decomposition (fermentation). Comparable processes are inherent to inorganic substances, for example, the formation of glass phases in clay during firing and the dissolution of crystal bonds of metals during melting. Heat often plays a special role in this process. Deliberate heating accelerates or even sets in motion transformational processes latent to material (Fitzenreiter, 2014). Examples are the drying of wood and foodstuffs, that is, the evaporation of cell water. Forced heat supply sets in motion transformations of the microstructure, which ultimately leads to new things with properties that are fundamentally different from those of the raw materials, for example, by changing protein molecules during roasting, boiling, frying, and baking; or by restructuring the crystal lattice during the firing of clay or melting of metal.

Technical interventions with materiality may be the combination of various procedures. In case of foodstuffs, for instance, hunting (= killing) or harvesting is followed by preparation, while for inorganic substances, extraction is followed by processing. Drying serves to preserve foodstuffs made of plants, and bleeding, smoking, or salting those made from animals. Grinding, sieving, washing, and smelting process inorganic substances. By the time interaction reaches these stages, the materiality of the entity has changed, and its designation usually changes accordingly. For example, we no longer speak of plants and animals, but of food; no longer of earth or stone, but of clay or ore. More generally, we speak of *products*. The designation as a product expresses how – through interaction – material is transformed in its consistency, and from a cognitive point of view, how materiality has changed its quality. The product is recognised as being something different. These objects and substances are *creations* (*Erzeugnisse*); entities that would not exist without their creators. The creation of non-natural substances is at the heart of human intervention into the materiality of things. Examples include the preparation of cereal porridge and dough through the special treatment of crops, or the alteration of the composition of metal by alloying (bronze) or forging (steel).

To do this, instruments that support the body are used. As *tools*, these instruments expand and improve the possibilities of the human body. In addition to simple tools, to create new materials people need special *devices*; sophisticated tools for which there are no natural or bodily templates, for example, mixing vessels and whisks, moulds and ovens, crucibles and anvils, looms, and so on. Tools and devices are media of technical interaction: they are, in the words of Marshall McLuhan (1964), 'extensions of man'. While tools are fundamentally determined by people in their use, devices tend to prescribe to people the actions to be performed. In the case of the machine, the most developed device, humans only act as operators in a process dictated by the machine (Marx, 1962: 328; Fitzenreiter, 2020: 403–410).[8]

3.1.2 Culture

The production, preparation, and consumption of food is a central feature of human interaction with its wider environment. The materiality of stuffs that serve as food is purposefully changed by a plethora of procedures to improve exploitability. Availability is ensured by the cultivation of plants and the keeping, domestication, and breeding of animals, as well as by techniques of preservation and low-loss storage. There are techniques of preparation intended to give access to the widest possible range of nutrients, such as cooking and fermentation. Others aim to produce food that is durable, transportable, and easy to consume, including drying, canning, and precooking. Finally, techniques of consumption appropriate to the consistency of the food reduce loss and, at the same time, play important social roles, for example, through the use of cutlery, tableware, and a menu sequence (Parker Pearson, 2003). Each practice is accompanied by the invention of tools and devices, along with the development of techniques for how these tools and devices are to be used.

The range of possible interactions with food, and the outcomes of these, draws attention to the reciprocity of interaction. Objects, materials, and tools not only react to human intervention, but stimulate, and sometimes force or determine, ways of human interference. To be consumed, the material consistency of each food requires special techniques of procurement, storage, preparation, and ingestion. Tools and devices require special techniques of operation which have to be acquired. Operating a plough, grinding in a mill, and eating with knife and fork have to be learned. During interaction, objects play the role of actants, and have an agency or affordance that stimulate certain modes of action; that is, objects act as things (Fox, Panagiotopoulos, & Tsouparopoulou, 2015). A knife, for example, 'forbids' anyone to grasp it by the blade.

---

[8] For an approach to technology via media-theory see: McLuhan, 1964; Kittler, 1985; Blumenberg, 2009. For perspectives on tools and their roles as 'extended phenotype' in evolutionary theory in archaeology see: O'Brien, Michael & Lee Lyman, 2000; Prentiss, 2019; for recent studies on change in archaeology: Crellin, 2020.

In the course of such interaction, materials change their ontological status by changing their names, and so do people. As the saying goes: 'You are what you eat' (in German, even more suggestively: 'Man ist, was man isst'; Feuerbach, 1975: 263). To this must be added: *how* one eats, *how* one prepares, and so on. A person's materiality – be it physical, social, or spiritual – is transformed during and by interaction. Hunting techniques and instruments make the hunter, techniques of cultivation make the farmer, and so on. ANT discusses this phenomenon of interactional reciprocity as a process of *hybridisation* (Latour, 2005), while in archaeology the term *entanglement* is generally preferred (Hodder, 2012; Stockhammer, 2013).[9]

The phenomenon of reciprocity – either hybrid or entangled – is of fundamental importance for understanding technical processes. Every interaction not only transforms the materiality of some object but has an effect on human agents, providing them with certain properties or qualities. These may be skills which are acquired, for example, by the use of tools such as a hammer or devices such as an oven. They may also be qualities gained through consumption, such as satiation by appropriate food or the practical-symbolic realisation of social status by using appropriate eating utensils. As when raw materials are transformed into products, such qualities are usually reflected in a new name or designation given to the human actor: they become peasants or bakers, gourmets or gourmands, noblemen or ascetics – in short, hybrids.

In addition to these more or less individual types of hybridisation, there are more general forms of interaction that affect large groups of people; for example, when (almost) all of a given community eat bread (and not porridge) or use a special type of cup. A network of things (bread, cup) and people constituted this way not only produces hybrids of an occupational group (bakers and potters), but entire societies (bread eaters / cup drinkers). Food and tools to consume food define belonging – that is, identity – in a practical, comprehensible way, experienced by each individual. Eating communities create identity in self-perspective, but equally present this identity to others. The extent to which identity can be created through interactions with food is demonstrated powerfully by food taboos or bans

---

[9] There is a certain vagueness in use of these terms. I follow Latour, 2005 when speaking of 'hybridisation' and resulting 'hybrids' as an ontological phenomenon of a thing-human interaction. Stockhammer, 2013, looking for typological features of archaeological evidence, defines the concept of 'material entanglement' of objects which elude 'pure' typology; for example, through the presence of 'foreign' features. Archaeological 'tanglegrams' as presented by Hodder, 2012 combine typological features of material culture ('material entanglement') and social aspects of human-thing relationship ('hybridisation') and include (shifts of) time and space. See the summary of recent usage of terms in: Budka, 2020, 411–14.

(Douglas, 1966; Volokhine, 2019), where deliberate avoidance of specific foods defines identity as a demarcation from others. Culture – the specific mode of human existence – is the outcome of human–thing interaction.

3.1.3 Archaeology

The phenomena described up to this point are constituted by practice and may only be grasped in practice. Hybridity is (mostly) a matter of the moment and identities have to be lived, experienced, and ascribed concretely; they are only real in the moment of interaction. As remarked in the Introduction, this immediate moment of practice is inaccessible to archaeologists. The archaeological record preserves only the material side of interaction, enshrining only a memory of interaction of things with people (Meskell, 2004). But these finds are still of course testimonies of interactions. Products indicate that there were people who acted as producers and consumers; tools and devices point to people who used them. Thus, on the one hand, we are able to explore technical doings and so to write a history of techniques, and on the other, we can recognise the kinds of hybrids shaped during people–thing interactions, and write cultural history. The possibility of identifying people who once gained identity by hybridisation makes it additionally possible to recognise similarities and differences at a communal level. Likewise, it becomes possible to interpret ambiguities in the evidence as indicators of inhomogeneity within a cultural spectrum and of social dynamics (Bader, 2021a). Material complexes are thus the remnants of countless interactions in which they were societalised with people, constituting an actor–network in which these things 'assembled' people.

3.2 Case Study: Bread, Beer, and Pots

3.2.1 Bread and Beer

One characteristic feature of Pharaonic culture is the widespread use of a range of plant-based foodstuffs, summarised in script as 'bread [and] beer' (*ta / henqet*; t ḥnḳ.t) (Samuel, 2000). In an intra-cultural perspective, the term is used as an archetypal designation for food; even more generally for provision and sustenance. Every offering to the dead opens with the wish for 'bread [and] beer' (Figure 9) and measures of bread and beer served as means of payment for workers, and of equivalating value (Warden, 2014: 31–51).

Made from fermented bruised grain by a technique that belongs to a broader African horizon of food preparation (van Wolputte & Fumanti, 2010), Pharaonic 'bread [and] beer' differed significantly in constituents and production from the bread prevalent in Egypt today.[10] Wheat (*triticum aestivum*; eg.: *sut* / sw.t), which can be easily processed into a solid dough and baked in an oven because of its high gluten content, was not initially available in Egypt. Rather, emmer (*triticum dicoccum*; eg.: *bedet* / bd.t) and barley (*hordeum*; eg.: *it* / jt) were used. Due to their low gluten content, these are more suitable for liquid doughs (Samuel, 1996; Florès, 2015: 267–305). To make them consumable, emmer and barley were malted, and the malt was then processed to form either bread or beer.

Pictorial and material evidence allows for a reconstruction of the *chaîne opératoire* (Vandier, 1964: 272–318; Faltings, 1998) (Figure 4). After preparatory pounding, rubbing, and scoring (?) of grain, the intermediate process of malting is then initiated (Faltings, 1995). The treated grain is referred to as *besha*-malt (bš(ꜣ)) in the inscriptions and thus conceptually distinguished as a product from cereals. This intermediate product was ground and sifted to a flour (*dj(u) dju* / ḏ(w)ḏw) of desired fineness, and out of this either a liquid dough (*shedjet* / (šḏt) or a kneaded dough (*pesen* / pzn) was produced. The former was poured into moulds and baked to form cone bread (*heta* or *hetjet* / ḥtꜣ / ḥtt), while kneaded dough was baked to form a flatbread called *pesen* (pzn). Also known, but not well documented, is the more complicated preparation, with the addition of sourdough (?), of a liquid dough which had to rise before it was baked in *setjet*-moulds (stt). A striking feature of the baking technique is that ovens were not used; rather, baking was done indirectly.[11] For this, ceramic containers were arranged in stacks and heated by a fire lit within (Verhoeven, 1984: 190–204). Liquid dough was either poured into these heated baking moulds (*bedja* or *setjet* /bḏꜣ, stt) or applied to a heated baking plate (*aperet* / ꜥpr.t). In addition to the three types of bread mentioned above, many others are attested; Coralie Schwechler (2020), for instance, analyses a total of forty-four designations for bread and pastry.

Besha malt was used not only for baking bread: when mixed with water, it also provided the base for beer production.[12] Texts document the addition of

---

[10] For the current state of research on the introduction of cereals in the Lower and Middle Nile Valley, see Fuller & Lucas, 2020. It remains striking that emmer, also widespread in the Near East (Meeks, 2006: 3), was commonly used instead of the 'African' staple sorghum, a type of millet. As it is often the case, Egypt technologically represents an Asian–African technological bridge or, culturally, a 'shifting scape' (Appadurai, 1996).

[11] Compare the findings from the bakery of Heit el-Ghurab in Giza: Lehner, 1996. Indirect baking on heated plates and shallow bowls may be seen as a refinement of the archaic baking technique on hot stones or in ashes, which is illustrated in funerary chapels by the so-called 'shepherd's flat bread' (Faltings, 1998: 232–54). Baking moulds are introduced only in Naqada III (late fourth millenium BCE) and are at first shallow bowls, only gradually changing to conical tubes (Hendrickx et al., 2002).

[12] Views differ regarding steps of processing. An older view, based on comparison with a recent Egyptian drink called *bouza* in which baked bread is added to the brewing mass, is presented in Helck, 1971. A different approach without the addition of baked bread is described by Samuel, 1996 and Faltings, 1998: 185–225.

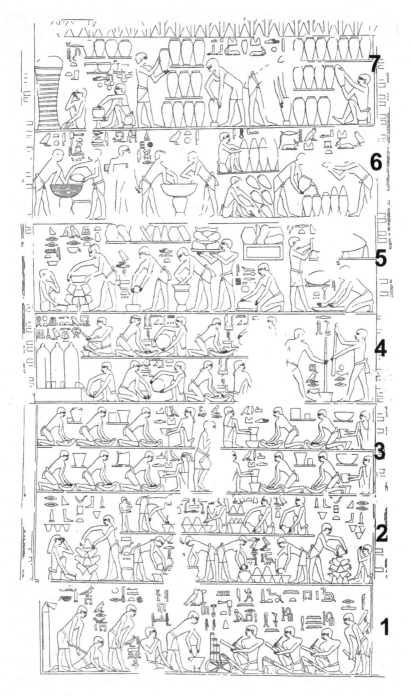

Figure 4 Baking, brewing and pottery production; west wall of Room II of the
funerary complex of Ti at Saqqara, c. 2400 BCE.

The tableau is composed of seven registers. A central panel, No. 4, displays the
production of the basic substance, *besha* malt (bš). To the left, a ration of grain is

dates, which served as flavouring agents and influenced the fermentation process as suppliers of yeast and sugar. According to pictorial representations, a person standing and trampling in a giant vat or people handling large sieves tamped and mixed the malt. Ambient heat initiated natural

---

Caption for Figure 4 (cont.)

taken from the granary and recorded by a scribe, and on the right it is tamped. In the middle, four groups are busy measuring (ḥȝt), triturating (tjšs), and scoring (? / nk) the *besha* malt. The lower sections, No. 3 and No. 2, depict the preparation of cone bread. Supervised by an overseer, women grind and sift (sȝj) grain (3); below them, on the right and on the left, a stack of *bedja* bread moulds is being heated, and in the centre liquid dough (šḏ.t) is poured into pre-heated moulds (2). Some moulds are covered for baking. In a sub-register above, two people perform an action with a stick (piercing / firming? sšr / smn), while two more people remove breads from moulds (wȝḥ.t). The lowest strip, No. 1, shows the overseer being driven to the registry, while scribes note down the delivery. Above the scene of malting, panel No. 5 depicts the preparation of other types of bread. On the far right, one person is taking *set* grain (zt; wheat? sprouted grain?) from a pot, while below, another person is preparing fresh (wȝḏ) dough (or sprouting grains?). To the left is a representation of 'beating' / kneading (sk) *pesen* dough (pzn) into flatbread, which is then carried away (to rise?). A vat then is filled (dnt) with (sour-?) dough poured through a sieve to prepare the dough mixture, and placed into a mould in the subsequent sequence. A stack of *setjet* moulds (stt) is heated on the right. Apparently, two moulds were placed on top of each other for large *setjet* loaves, as indicated by the double-cone shape of some bread sitting on top of a shelf and by the fact that the mould being taken from the stack is called the 'bottom of the loaf' (ḥr.t t). The upper two strips illustrate beer production. No. 6, to the left, depicts the mixing of mash with other substances, the scene replacing the usual image of a brewer scrunching mash in a vat with his feet. Filtration through a sieve is depicted in the ensuing scene. To the right, there follows the smearing of beer jugs with clay; the jugs are then filled and sealed. In the uppermost panel (No. 7), the production of the required vessels is shown, with jars formed by hand on the right, and on the left a person throwing a vessel on a potter's wheel. On the far left, a ceramic kiln is being operated.

Source: graphic from Épron & Daumas, 1939: pl. LXVI, reworked by the author.

fermentation of the prepared mash (*ah* / ꜣḥ). For filtration, the mash was pressed through a basket sieve and the liquid collected in a vessel before being poured into jugs and sealed with a clay stopper. Different varieties were defined in terms of additives, strength, or colour, and each was again individually labelled (Helck, 1971: 43–52).

Most representations of food production of the kind described above come from funerary decoration, which tends to reproduce ideal, seemingly static, technologies.[13] In reality, the exchange of knowledge between people and things leads to constant changes. From the Middle Kingdom (early second millennium BCE) onwards, liquid dough is no longer attested. Rather pre-kneaded pieces of dough were inserted into conical baking moulds (Schwechler, 2020: 249–51; Bats, 2020). Moulds were also now significantly narrower and longer (Jacquet-Gordon, 1981). Since baking bread this way, which is effective for liquid doughs, is less efficient for solid doughs, by the New Kingdom (late second millennium) at the latest, individually heated baking moulds seem to have been replaced by substantial cylindrical ovens, allowing the production of a large number of baked goods at one time (Samuel, 2000: 566; Depraetere, 2002; Ryan, 2016: 32–34). Likewise, new techniques for beer production can be traced in which portions of the mash were heated to control fermentation and make a brew that could be preserved for longer (Samuel, 2000: 540).

3.2.2 Ceramics

While the actual foodstuffs tend to leave only sparse traces in the archaeological record, instruments of production and consumption associated with them are often made of more durable materials. Through them, it is possible to access something of the temporal and spatial concreteness of technical processes and how things (and people) change (Warden, 2014; Warden, 2021). Furthermore, tools and devices used in food production (and elsewhere) are examples of the interplay of materials and techniques. On the one hand, these should contribute to an increase in quality and quantity of the product they are used to procure, and on the other, they should generally be as cost effective to manufacture as possible. This tension between effectiveness of use and costs of production is fundamental to the concept of material transformation.

---

[13] When considering the apparent staticity of funerary decoration, we should be cautious to read it as an illustration of (lack of) technical progress, when it may reflect deliberately old-fashioned ways of production that were appropriate in the frame of funerary cult (Fitzenreiter, 2020: 211–38). See the wide range of bread and pastry designations suggesting also a great variety of baking techniques (Schwechler, 2020).

In archaeology, change in the materiality of pottery over a long time has been perceived primarily as a feature of typology that can be used in dating an archaeological context, with far less attention given to the dynamics of how and why vessel shapes changed (French, 2016; Bader, 2021b). One pioneering study here is that of Stephan Seidlmayer (2000), in which material change itself is the focus of investigation. Seidlmayer's study opens with the analysis of a ceramic assemblage from the northwest of Elephantine town, dating from the Old to Middle Kingdoms (second half of the third millennium BCE). This shows that fine light red marl clays that dominated in the early Old Kingdom are replaced by medium–fine Nile silts with a red coating at the end of this period. This shift is correlated by Seidlmayer with changing production conditions: although marl clay is of higher quality, it has significantly higher production costs, both in material procurement and in processing and firing. Such an elaborate product could become a common commodity only under a highly centralised authority such as the Old Kingdom's early state, which was able to maintain production and distribution centres and to ensure storage and transport of raw materials, as well as of the finished products. With the loss of control over distribution channels, ceramic production regionalised at the end of the Old Kingdom. Accordingly, the later spectrum is dominated by local resources, featuring products that require less effort in production, including the amount of firing required. Thus, networks of needs and expenditure on both sides of a human–thing network influenced change in technical interaction as well as in material evidence.

Seidlmayer then examines changes in shape of closed ceramic types (Figure 5). From the Naqada period (fourth millennium BCE) to the end of the Fifth Dynasty (mid-third millennium BCE), ovoid-shaped jars with a high shoulder are typical, but this changes quite abruptly at the beginning of the Sixth Dynasty. From this time on, the vessel's centre of gravity lay much lower. Seidlmayer attributes this change in shape to a new technique of vessel production. The early types were produced by manually raising the body of the vessel, resulting in a narrow foot and a high-set vessel shoulder. After the introduction of the potter's wheel during the Fifth Dynasty, the body was thrown out of the base, and thus the centre of gravity remained in the lower part of the vessel. What is highly interesting is the time lag of about 200 years between the introduction of the potter's wheel during the Fifth Dynasty and the result change in vessel shape – an 'exchange of knowledge' between things and people – in the Sixth Dynasty. The outer shape of the vessel, a kind of expression of human will and knowledge, was only gradually adapted to a new technique, which in a way 'demanded' a new shape. Information from the world of things was to be experienced first, and – after a phase of uncertainty and a change of paradigm – transferred into conceptual solutions, in this case an outer shape that was more appropriate to the mode of

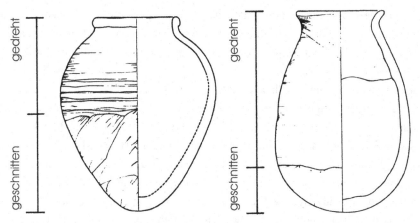

Figure 5 Changes in pottery styles resulting from the introduction of the potter's wheel. Left: vessel type common up to the Fifth Dynasty / c. 2300 BCE; lower half handmade, upper half wheel-thrown. Right: vessel type common during Sixth Dynasty / after 2300 BCE; only the lower third is handmade, the upper two-thirds are wheel-thrown.
Source: Seidlmayer, 2000: Abb. 5; drawing: William Schenck / © DAI Kairo; graphic: Stephan Seidlmayer / © Stephan Seidlmayer; reproduced with permission.

technical intervention. It must have been accompanied by a cognitive process of accepting the resulting shape as appropriate or, in conceptual terms, as 'beautiful'. Only perception during a phase of habituation makes the new become the typical.

Finally, Seidlmayer looks at a common type of food ceramic, so-called 'beer jars', from the perspective of their function (see Figure 4, for production (7) and use (6)). These jars are of approximately uniform size, manufactured by hand from a coarse ceramic mass, and apparently used only once. A characteristic feature is a smear of fine Nile mud applied to the inside after firing (Faltings, 1998: 204 f). Since these pots are leaky due to their simple manufacture, they were caulked this way just before they were filled. The method is extremely cost-saving and at the same time effective; Seidlmayer compares it to the use of modern composite materials in which one component ensures strength and the other one tightness. Hence, this extraordinary object type reflects knowledge exchange on different material components, resulting in a technical procedure that enables high-volume but cost-effective production. It was only common at large-scale breweries, namely, in production centres that had an enormous output and did not factor in the return of used vessels. The beer jars thus represent a kind of ancient disposable packaging (Faltings, 1991: 116).[14]

---

[14] However, see Hendrickx et al., 2002: 293, n. 104 for possible reuse.

3.3 Culture as Practice

A next step of an archaeology of technology is to move on to the human–thing hybrids constituted by people's interactions with materiality and thus ultimately to people. In his description of Egypt, Herodotus (II, 77) characterises Egyptians as 'bread eaters' (*artophagoi* / αρτοφαγοι) (Schwechler, 2020: XI) and in Aeschylus's *Danaids* the boast is made that Greeks – unlike Egyptians – do not drink (sloppy) beer (*zytos* / ζυθος), but are real men (drinking wine) (Helck, 1971: 15).[15] Characteristic food is a characteristic of people. The Egyptians' funerary wish to be provided with 'bread [and] beer' testifies that in Pharaonic self-perception food 'made' people in a comparable way. A major feature of Pharaonic Egyptian identity is the provision – in life and death – of 'bread [and] beer'.

Stereotypical attributions – such as the demand for bread and beer – paint, on the surface, a picture of static cultural boundaries. Similarly to features marking typologies of material culture – pots, tools, jewellery, and so on – humans are seemingly to be segregated into groups with typological characteristics, into 'tribes', 'peoples', and 'nations' (Matić, 2020: 8). However, the constant movement of typological features reveals a multi-layered network of inter-actions and material entanglements. On the one hand, there are factors that determine quite stable patterns of interaction between people and things, such as the species of grain cultivated in the Nile Valley and the deposits of clay available. And yet it is against this stable backdrop that change becomes apparent, leading to sometimes fundamental alterations. Liquid doughs are replaced by solid doughs; ceramic masses are quite different in administrative centres from those of local production. Much debated are cases of 'material entanglement' (Stockhammer, 2013), when typological features traditionally attributed to 'foreign' cultural clusters are mixed with, and appear in contexts attributed to, Pharaonic culture, as in the case of the 'enigma of the Hyksos' (Bader, 2021a; Mourad, 2021) or the 'colonisation' of Nubia (Smith, 2020). In contrast to the static models of typology – interpreting a limited set of material features as a *culture* – ANT speaks of networks of entangled actors as the very mode of existence of the social and the cultural as well: a sphere where things and people 'assemble'. Interacting this way, things and people create networks of social organisation, such as central state versus local domains, where differ-ences in accessibility of materials and manual labour shape differences in the materiality of things. They create networks of technical interaction, when the stimuli of the potter's wheel affects in turn the shape of vessels. They create

---

[15] On the identity-forming role of food cultures in ancient Greece, see Beck, 2020: 82–92. See also designations like *ichthyophagoi* (fish-eaters) and *elephantophagoi* (elephant-eaters) that Greek geographers such as Agatharchides used when describing foreign people (Burstein, 1989).

networks of cost and benefit that lead to economic optimisation. And they create networks of material entanglement that indicate social mobility, 'third spaces', and the ambiguity of identities (Bhabha, 2004). For an example of the latter, we might turn to temples dedicated to the 'Pharaonic' god Amun in the Sudanese Kingdom of Kush, where conical bread moulds were deposited in enormous quantity in the second half of the first millennium BCE (Anderson & Ahmed, 2006) (Figure 6). Notably, these moulds are not attested elsewhere in the Sudan, whether in temples of local gods, funerary areas, or settlement contexts, and nor are they found in contemporaneous Egypt (Jacquet-Gordon, 1981: 21). We might see in these moulds evidence of a particular practice of preparing the customary 'white bread offering' to Pharaonic gods in a 'Pharaonic' fashion.

Figure 6 'Pharaonic-style' offering: A heap of conical bread moulds at the Amun Temple of Jebel Barkal, Sudan, for a 'white bread offering' to deities of the Pharaonic pantheon in the Kingdom of Kush (first millennium BCE). **Source:** photograph from 2017 by J. R. Anderson, reproduced with permission (© J.R. Anderson).

However, using the indirect baking technique (or just imitating it?), the rolls were baked in a way no longer common in Egypt at the time, and using a dough prepared from millet (*durra*) that was also not known from Egypt. An adapted and transformed baking technique became an invented tradition, a custom that 'assembled' people and things to build a religious community, maybe Pharaonic in content, but quite local in essence (for this see Section 6). It is the primacy of practice over phenomena that becomes obvious in such cases, reminding us of the demand of Pierre Bourdieu (1977: 72):

'In order to escape the realism of the structure, which hypothesizes systems of objective relations by converting them into totalities already constituted outside of the individual history and group history, it is necessary to pass from the *opus operatum* to *modus operandi*, from statistical regularity, or algebraic structure to the principle of the production of this observed order, and to construct the theory of practice, or, more precisely, the theory of the mode of generation of practices, which is the precondition of establishing an experimental science of the *dialectic of the internalization of externality and the externalization of internality*, or more simply, of incorporation and objectification.'

4 Technology and Conceptualisation: Craft

4.1 Skill, Knowledge, and the Communication of Knowledge

The technical process involves not just the transformation of raw materials but also the cognitive apperception of the ongoing process itself. There is often a retarding moment in this process, as the realisation of new technical possibilities tends to emerge only after a period of human adaptation. The previous section mentioned the example of the potter's wheel inspiring, after a delay, a new type of vessel shape. Technical change inspired by things on the one side requires change in human behaviour on the other. This adaptation is a collective one, as it is not only producers who have to get used to new processes and products, but consumers too. Perhaps most importantly, other steps of technical interaction have to be adjusted as well: things also have to get used to the new.

Consciously performed interaction therefore requires a high degree of knowledge exchange between things and people. This exchange manifests itself in experiences gained by practical action; in other words, as skills (Sennet, 2008; Kuijpers, 2018). Such skills can only be experienced and learned individually as tacit knowing (Polanyi, 1966). Skills are incorporated, and become a physical expression of the above-discussed process of hybridisation of things and people. They are a kind of an imprint of things which leave their mark on people. Skill may express itself simply in a certain dexterity that experience provides, but it can also produce a conspicuous imprint in the body. If particular techniques are routinely performed, the body adapts and becomes trained or deformed, depending on one's point of view (Zakrzewski, Shortland, & Rowland, 2016: 150–8). Physical features shaped in the course of interaction stand as stereotypical images of the hybrid that emerges out of thing and human. They symbolise both the human being – who as a hybrid is characterised not only by the instruments they use but also by their own physical constitution: as a scarred blacksmith or a well-fed baker – and also stand as personifications of techniques, such as the graceful muses who act as images of music, dance, and storytelling. And they serve as images of the Other, the counterpart of interaction, like Pharaonic fecundity figures, whose corpulence represents nature's abundance and fertility (Baines, 1985) (Figure 7).

Figure 7 A body shaped by and to represent abundance and fertility. Fecundity figure from the temple of Sammanud (Sebennytos) (New York, Metropolitan Museum of Art; Rogers Fund, 1912; Accession Number: 12.182.4b); c. 350 BCE. **Source:** www.metmuseum.org/art/collection/search/551787.

Skill is ability gained from individual experience. It is always specific, related to a particular technique and Other; whether to cereals, to clay, or to metal. Skill cannot be passed on. Knowledge, on the other hand, is a product of 'mental work' and may in turn be shared. To transform individual skill into exchangeable knowledge, techniques of conceptualisation have to be developed, as well as respective media. To transmit knowledge, gestures may be used. This may take the form of training in certain movements, which are demonstrated and then imitated and so passed on as knowledge; consider the hand movements of a potter, dance steps, or drills for warfare. Sound can serve similarly; for instance, through training to recognise different material properties. Metal sounds different from wood, high-fired ceramics sound different to those that are low-fired, and so on. Other phonetic forms of knowledge transmission include the teaching of songs, verses, narratives, and, finally, oral instruction itself. Moves and dance steps are incorporated by transmission and materialised by repetition; speech is memorised and retold; and, finally, images and writings are placed and used on a wide variety of host materials (Kehnel & Panagiotopoulos, 2015). Each of these manifestations of knowledge, whether materialised in a move, a sound, or even an object, represents a 'medium of erudition': an epistemic thing (for this see Section 5), in which knowledge has met a manifestation that can be transmitted, either because it is audible, visible, or otherwise repeatable (sounds, demonstration, moves), or because it is permanent (image, writing).

Entangled with a medium, materialised knowledge possesses two aspects. First, it itself is an instrument that serves as a tool during interaction, as an 'extension of man('s brain)'. By medially eternalised knowledge, technique is professionalised: those who acquire previous knowledge by studying books or practising demonstrated techniques interact faster and more successfully.[16] At the same time, these media of externalised knowledge are themselves things to be interacted with, are able to transcend knowledge passed on from producers, and transgress time and space. In order to interact with these media, specific techniques are again developed and a distinct technology of knowledge transfer is established. Reading a book, a sheet of music, or a blueprint are skills to be learned, in the same way, in fact, as archaeologists learn to 'read' the past in the surviving evidence.

If knowledge is materialised in these media, it can be passed on, unlike skill and experience itself. It operates in smaller or larger circles and as such forms

---

[16] As a result, people who acquire a high level of knowledge through media (and often a much lower level of skill earned by actual interaction) tend to underestimate the agency of the Other – the things – and perceive themselves (or humans in general) as the sole actor/s. But if the knowledge is insufficient or wrong, the other side may strike back cruelly: in the form of an accident (Kassung, 2009).

actor–networks out of the people it co-entangles. These can be considered knowledge communities, academic schools, or 'communities of values'; that is, all forms of social assemblages in which knowledge as an epistemic thing (about right and wrong, good and evil, etc.) binds people. This is how 'styles of thought' and paradigms are generated, as Thomas Kuhn (1970: 10) describes the 'normal science':

"normal science' means research firmly based upon one or more past scientific achievements, achievements that some particular scientific community acknowledges for a time as supplying the foundation for its further practice.... Aristotle's Physica, Ptolemy's Almagest, Newton's Principia and Opticks, Franklin's Electricity, Lavoisier's Chemistry, and Lyell's Geology – these and many other works served for a time implicitly to define the legitimate problems and methods of a research field for succeeding generations of practitioners'.

Materialised knowledge is produced as a distinct creation for distribution and consumption, as with other products. Knowledge is often a rare commodity and able therefore to be monopolised. Even through non-verbalised experiences, experienced technicians may market themselves better than those with less aptitude, or be marketed better by those who exercise social control; it is usually not the blacksmith who is king, but the one who controls the blacksmith. That is why it is also worthwhile to keep knowledge scarce. In a way, this scarcity of knowledge is guaranteed by thresholds of medial techniques. Only those who master the vocabulary of the paradigm – its technical terminology and decorum – are able to participate in the exchange of knowledge. A technical terminology which to the layperson often seems mysterious is a phenomenon quite typical of knowledge production. Scientific language, sociolects, and sophisticated media all serve as techniques of segregation, as do regulations placed on physical accessibility to media, whether writings, concepts, or people.

4.2 Case Study: Metallurgy

4.2.1 The Lost-Wax Process

Metallurgical processes are often shrouded in an aura of mystery, stemming from the use of powerful heat sources, the striking transformations that can occur, and the rarity and high value of raw materials and products. It is not for nothing that hermetic sciences such as alchemy are based to a considerable degree on practices originating in metallurgy (Eliade, 1978). In Pharaonic Egypt, lost-wax casting was widely used in the production of figurative objects (Bianchi & Ziegler, 2014; Fitzenreiter et al., 2014). Due to the preservation of a considerable number of finds (Roeder, 1956; Weiss, 2012; Tiribilli, 2018) and a set of semi-finished products (Fitzenreiter, Willer, & Auenmüller, 2016;

Auenmüller, Verly, & Rademakers, 2019), we are fairly well informed, in particular, about Egyptian bronze casting in the middle of the first millennium BCE (Figure 8).

To start the lost-wax process, a model of the object to be cast is made from a wax mixture, either by hand or by pouring liquefied wax into a mould. Moulds for various products are well known in Egypt, including the indirect baking techniques described in the previous section. The terms used are identical: *bedja* or *bet* (bḏȝ / bt) refer to 'mould' in general. Next, the wax model is provided with a sprue system – a channel – built in wax and then embedded in a ceramic mass. Experience in ceramic production is helpful in creating this unusual casing, which requires somewhat contradictory properties. On the one hand, the material has to be fine enough to mould even the smallest details of a wax model; on the other, it must also be strong enough to withstand the pressure from molten

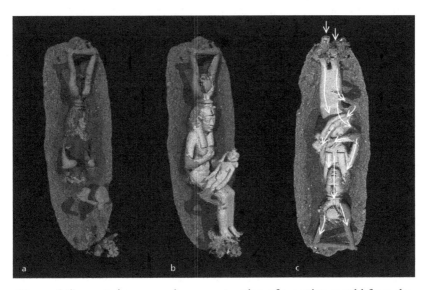

Figure 8 Computed tomography reconstruction of a casting mould from the Qubbet el-Hawa; c. 550–400 BCE.
a) Section through the mould, the wall of which is composed of up to four layers of differently mixed ceramics. Marked in red are metal residues indicating an unsuccessful casting.
b) Virtual flooding of the negative space in yellow, revealing the statuette of Isis with the Horus child intended for casting.
c) Reconstruction of a casting process: metal would have flowed into the mould through a sprue at the feet. Connecting channels added at the feet of the child Horus, the elbow of Isis, and between the horns of the crown would ensure circulation of melted metal.
Source: reconstruction by F. Willer / D. Meinel, after: Fitzenreiter, Willer, & Auenmüller, 2016: Figure 7.41; reproduced with permission.

metal flowing in. At the same time, the mass should be elastic in order to absorb expansion, and should be permeable to air to dissipate gas at the moment of casting. Finally, it has to be easily detachable from the blank after casting. To ensure these properties, masses of different mixtures are applied in several layers on the wax model in order to create a composite material which combines components with distinct properties. The prepared mould then is hardened by firing, while the wax model is burnt out. After that, molten metal is poured into the resultant negative space, and after cooling, the mould is broken and the blank is taken out to be reworked mechanically.

The lost-wax technique includes several technical steps which are conceptually quite demanding. In particular, the successive existence of the object in three *material* dimensions – as a wax model, as a negative space, and finally as a piece of metal – is often difficult for laypeople to comprehend. Even today, metalworkers are not always fully informed about all of the processes concerning decrystallisation and recrystallisation during the stages of melting and cooling. Nonetheless, for laypeople as well as for practitioners, the primacy of practice applies: anyone who has only once carried out a casting, or even just experienced it as a spectator, gets a feeling for the process and a glimpse of knowledge.

4.2.2 Dissemination

Only a few people, however, have had occasion and the opportunity to gain experience in metallurgy. In metallurgy, materials and devices require technical specialisation built up along a *chaîne opératoire*: there are miners and smelters responsible for processing raw materials, and founders and forgers who transfer raw metals into finished workpieces. These processes are almost never done at the same place and time, and so intermediaries are also called upon, including traders, contractors, and warehouse personnel. Actor–networks formed this way are spatially and temporally expanded, reaching from the copper mines of Sinai and Cyprus to the smelting places of Aswan, or from the tin deposits of Britain to the lead pits of Greece (Tylecote, 1992). Once extracted, metal is recycled again and again and in different places; even a component of a contemporary device may be made of copper mined three thousand years ago.

Networks like that of the metallurgical *chaîne opératoire* extend into time and space. They not only promote the dissemination of materials and products, they also promote the transfer of knowledge (Burmeister et al., 2013). In the latter, the role of people is often overestimated, and that of things underrated. Flows of people (and their knowledge) are preceded by flows of things (and their knowledge). It is the thing that attracts interest, as people try to take possession of it or to imitate it, and so it 'assembles' people into networks of knowledge. Every object, because of the knowledge materialised in it, is a medium that passes on this knowledge. By interacting with things that have 'come down' this way, human actors acquire new experiences and establish new techniques. New things pass on new knowledge. Such a model of a 'disconnected' knowledgescape (Sjaastad, 2018), where knowledge is spread and inspired by materials and things, is much more appropriate to archaeological evidence than is the master narrative of monolocal 'inventions' and their dissemination by rambling wise men – one of these epics rooted in the myth of the culture hero and still cultivated by modern patent law.[17]

4.2.3 Specialists: The Stela of the Artist Irtisen

To us, the abilities and skills of Pharaonic metalworkers are for the most part documented only by the objects themselves. Classic Egyptological studies of the lost-wax process such as Roeder (1933) and Schorsch (1988) read and record from these objects the techniques, skills, mastery, and failure of individuals. But these individuals remain as anonymous as the bakers, brewers, and potters from the previous section. Nonetheless, there is some pictorial and textual evidence which not only informs about technical detail and practice, but in some cases allows the protagonists themselves to emerge. The stela of Irtisen, probably from Abydos and dating to the late Eleventh Dynasty (c. 2000 BCE) is one example (Figure 9). Its inscription has been studied several times and offers glimpses of an extraordinary personality (Schenkel, 1965: 245–49; Barta, 1970; Barbotin, 2005: 56 f.; Bryan, 2017; Stauder, 2018; Fitzenreiter, 2019; Nyord, 2020: 36 f.).

The stela is decorated in its lower part with a scene not uncommon for objects of this kind. In front of Irtisen and his wife Hepu, descendants headed by the eldest son, Senwosret, perform a funerary offering. The couple is shown once more below, sitting in a shrine in front of an offering table. Both depictions define the stela as a medium of the funerary cult, the purpose of which is to ensure eternal contact between the deceased and their family as well as the eternal provision of the dead (sitting in their funerary installation). In a similarly traditional fashion, the inscription opens with the king's title and name, mentions the title and name of Irtisen, and has a detailed offering list. After a list of additional gifts connected to rituals particular to Abydos, the owner of the stela

---

[17] Compare the rich archaeological literature on innovation: Shortland, 2001; Wilde, 2003; Bourriau & Phillips, 2004; Rowley-Conwy, 2007; Maran & Stockhammer, 2017; Shaw, 2017; Burmeister & Bernbeck, 2017; Mourad, 2021. These examples do, however, often follow the *invention-and-dissemination-by-people* pattern – one that does not explain, for example, how knowledge of wax-casting reached the Americas in the first millennium BCE (von Schuler-Schörnig, 1972; Fitzenreiter, 2020: 164–76).

Figure 9 Stela of Irtisen, probably from Abydos, c. 2.000 BCE (Paris, Louvre C 14).
Source: drawing after Barta, 1970: Abb. 1.

himself starts to speak. While the text up to this point makes use of familiar phraseology, the section that follows records a hitherto unattested series of four utterances, all beginning with 'I know' and providing a kind of confessional self-description of Irtisen (Fischer-Elfert, 2002). In his first confession, Irtisen describes himself as an educated specialist who is both proficient in hieroglyphic writing and familiar with rituals associated with the production of pictorial works:

'I know the en/decoding of 'divine words' [= the hieroglyphs] [and] the performance of the rituals of the festivals. Every talent, [I am] endowed with it, without [any] of it escaping me. Verily, [I am] a craftsman who is excellent in his craft [and one who] excels by what he knows'.

The second confession is of particular interest, for Irtisen describes in artfully encoded language the process of lost-wax casting:[18]

'I know the parts [= the alloy components] of the sunken [= the molten metal] [and] the 'teetering / lifting of the head' [= a technical term for the visual assessment of the metal's melting equilibrium point, indicating readiness for casting, and / or a metaphor for lifting the crucible]; the calculation of the 'taken out' [= volume of the mould and, from this, the required amount of metal and / or the correct moment the mould is ready to be cast out] [and] the 'letting in as going out' [= burning out of the wax model to make room for the molten metal and / or pouring the metal out of the crucible into the mould] [so that] it [= the sunken / the molten metal] enters to come [= to fill the mould], [being] contained [= by the mould], towards its seat[ing] [= the solidification of the metal]'.

What follows is a list of poses of human figures, using a particularly 'pictorial' terminology quite appropriate to describe the artistry of lively depiction, going from simple to complex poses:

'I know the passing of a [male divine] image [and] the coming of a female image; the swinging [?] of the arms [= wings] of the 'bird of ten' [= image of the king slaying ten enemies raising their hands like wings of a bird; [cf. Figure 14]] [and] the wriggling [of] each of the [ten] slain; the 'looking of the eye to the other of its two pupils' [= squinting] [and] the being-in-fear of the face of the vigilant [= the central person of the 'bird of ten' who faces the spectator], the swaying of the arm of the 'excreted one' [in a faecal sense] [and] the ['hippopotamic'] staggering of the one running [away]'.

---

[18] Other translations have also been suggested; Brugsch (1880: 457f) was the first to see references to metal casting, followed by Barbotin (2005: 56). Baud (1938) assumes the cell fusion technique was used. In this and other translations, the quotation marks are used to highlight metaphorical terms or phrases – no such punctuation existed in the original.

In his last confession, Irtisen boasts to have made a register of either traditional objects or artistic rules and to have passed this knowledge on to his son.

'I know the making of a description of things that have come down to us [and so] not to cause [= prevent] them [= the things] from being burned by fire [and] being washed us away by water truly [therefore] no going out is [= seeking advice] because of that [= the 'things that have come down'] in any case except in front of me [for] I have always been alone – together with my eldest bodily son'.

Following the mentioning of the son, a passage states the actual reason for the erection of the stela. Here the king declares that the office of the father is to be passed to this son, who thus also receives the latter's status (and in turn is able and obliged to perform the sacrifice for his father):

'[Therefore] the God [= the king] commands: He [= the son] shall make [that] he goes out because of this [= shall take over the office of the father]! [For] I [= the king] have seen the 'going forth of his arms' [= the son's products] when he was chief of works in every precious material, from silver and gold to ivory and ebony'.

Finally, the wish for the funerary offerings is once again uttered, as illustrated by the depiction of the couple sitting in the shrine.

The message of this monument is quite complex, operating on a social, a religious and a technological level. Here, it stands as an example of how the conceptualisation of technical processes is tied to a particular style of thought. This is done in four 'confessions', describing a process of knowledge circulation on matters of the artist's craft, passed from father to son. Passing possessions and claims from one generation to the next is a topic otherwise common to funerary contexts, but this time it includes the transmission of encoded knowledge (or wisdom).

In his first confession, Irtisen presents himself as a rightful owner of this knowledge by referring both to the skill that is unique to him – his 'magical' talent (*heka* / ḥkȝ) – and to the knowledge he has acquired by learning (*rekh* / rḫ). The second confession links knowledge to practices of image making, appearing here in the guise of its most complicated technique: metal casting. The mode of expression is remarkable, with the drawing of allusions to the Osiris myth (Bryan, 2017: 5 f (e); Stauder, 2018: 260): the melting of the alloy is equated with the decay of the god, whose alias, 'the weary one' (= the sunken one), is cited. The equilibrium point of molten metal, which implies it has reached casting temperature – or the lifting of the crucible – is associated with the motif of 'lifting the head', initiating the revival of the god. Terms describing the casting process refer to the judgment and vindication of Osiris at the court of the gods, and evoke ideas of crossing the thresholds to and from the afterlife. Formation in a mould is equated with the re-joining of the dismembered god's limbs in bandages and the hardening of metal 'in its place' is paralleled with the reinstatement of the god 'on his [throne] seat'. By underpinning the technical process with mythological allusions, Irtisen not only uses metaphorical (technical) language, but the same moment interprets his craft as being part of a universal cycle of (re-)creation. Further, the operation is located within a paradigm which is communicable beyond technical specialists, since allusions to religious motifs are comprehensible by a broader public. While Irtisen refers to the Osiris rituals celebrated in Abydos, he is locating his narrative in the here and now, as well as in an eternal cycle of cultic regeneration – including his own.

This metaphorical description of transformation of substance is followed by that of acquisition of outer form. Underneath the seemingly burlesque description of various bodily poses, the spectacle of the destruction of Osiris's enemies staged dramatically in Abydos is alluded to. In the last confession, the motif of knowledge and experience is taken up again and, underpinned with allusions to local historical events such as the fairly recent destruction of the site by civil war, their transmission is thematised. This transmission of knowledge takes place not only via 'media of erudition' – in this case, an inventory written down by Irtisen – but also as 'secret' tacit knowing, transmitted only from father to son.

4.3 Media and Concept

The example of Irtisen shows how conceptualisations of knowledge exchange between things and people – a phenomenon which is defined as technology proper in this Element – is cast into concepts which are communicable within a specific cultural mindset. Part of this involves formulations that allow allusions to be understood not by everyone, but by those trained in this form of conceptualisation. Playful secrecy is part of the Pharaonic paradigm,[19] which is deeply rooted in a 'culture of ambiguity' that defies the Cartesian duality of western styles of thought (Bauer, 2011; Morenz, 2020). A monument like Irtisen's stela is not meant to be perceived by larger groups. To understand hieroglyphs, one must grasp their ambiguity (*se-sheta* / s:štꜣ) (Fitzenreiter, in press), a task not everyone is capable of. These kinds of media are not simply

---

[19] Comparable to the mythologically reworked description of the casting process by Irtisen is, among other examples, a hymn recorded on the walls of the Dendera temple in which the brewing of beer is mytho-poetically hyperbolised (Leitz, 2017). Religious texts abundantly reflect technical processes in a mytho-metaphorical, often even humoresque way (Guglielmi, 1991; Guglielmi, 1994).

tools for the transmission of knowledge. The corpus of concepts, formed by mythology and text, in itself is a kind of material that actors use to produce – and limit – ideas, concepts, and know-how. In the text of his stela, Irtisen and his entourage demonstrate their social position while the same moment creating this position on a cultural level. In terms of cultural positioning, it is remarkable to note how the materialisation of identity is achieved by formulations in which Irtisen confesses his familiarity – his hybridisation – with things as well as with techniques that entangle him with things. It is this kind of reflection of the entanglements between humans and things which enables people to recognise themselves (Quirke, 2018).

5 Technology, Environment, and Religion

5.1 Ontology, Epistemes, and Myth

Though techniques and technologies do not necessarily have to do with religion, aspects of religious practice have appeared here and there in previous sections. In the Kingdom of Kush, bread was baked in the cult of Amun, as things are produced that 'assemble' people in a religious congregation. As Irtisen on his stela conceptualises the transformation of substances with reference to Osirian mythology, technical experiences and religious concepts are associated in order to be 'thought' and understood within a community sharing a religiously inspired worldview. The creation of social groups as congregations or communities of faith can be seen as one of the most import-ant outcomes, or products, of religious practice (Durkheim, 1915). Yet the creation of the social group itself is not the actual goal of most religious practice, but more of an unconscious side effect. Religious practice and its techniques – prayers, chants, dances, sacrifices, almsgiving, fasting, and so on – primarily focuses on everyday tasks (as bread baking does) and on structuring life in the broadest sense. In the words of Robin Horton (1993: 6), religion is practised in order to obtain 'explanation, prediction and control'. It helps to understand what happens to people, it helps to predict what will happen, and it helps to control what happens.

The example of Irtisen's stela illustrates how broad the field of explanation, prediction, and control by means of religiously formulated concepts can be, and how this field extends into seemingly non-religious realms such as arts and crafts. To use, for example, metaphoric language to assure technical procedures by rituals and to clothe products in the language of ambiguity seems to be mysterious only for those not being actively included in the collective world-view at hand. Claude Lévi-Strauss (1962) and recently proponents of an onto-logical turn in anthropology (Haywood, 2017) point out that conceptualisation rests on epistemological foundations that may differ from one collective to another. People interact with the wider universe through different strategies, or techniques, of appropriation, which in turn lead to different experiences. Based on these experiences, phenomena and things are correlated with specific properties and those properties are not necessarily perceived in the same ways by people using other techniques of appropriation. Gifted with different properties, things become something different from, for example, contemporary western conceptualisations, or from what may have been proposed one or two paradigms before the prevailing one. What is god in the perspective of one cultural worldview may be nature in another; or, in an early modern perspective, both: *deus sive natura* (Spinoza, 1677: 4).

That different experiences lead to different concepts of the relationship between humans and environment is of central importance in any technologically inspired approach to ontology. It not only makes it possible to describe how and why the Other is perceived differently, it also reveals that differences in conceptualisations of the Other arise because it is itself only shaped, or produced, in the course of interaction. It is the process of cognitive appropriation that gives to any un-formatted and non-recognised 'being' a specific mode of existence. The Other is constituted of the recognition of properties it 'possesses' as a quality of its own kind (Hegel, 1975: 95). To recognise this ontological peculiarity implies that, just as human beings only constitute personhood and individuality by interaction with the Other (see Sections 3 and 4), likewise the Other exists only as a hybrid, generated precisely by this interaction with humans. Nature, too, only exists as a feature of the environment as qualified by interaction with, and thus hybridised to, humans (Latour, 1993).

On the basis of such interactions, *epistemes* are generated: concepts or forms of knowledge which stand for specific qualities and properties experienced during interaction with the Other. Such epistemes are bases for further interaction and thus keep the system of epistemes in motion (Cancik-Kirschbaum & Traninger, 2015). Although experience is fluid and diverse, recurring impressions generate knowledge with a specific kind of materiality or object, becoming an *epistemic thing*. Existing on a conceptual level independent of an actual experience, the episteme may be used to qualify or be attributed to unlimited 'Others'. Epistemes created out of the recognition of such abstract qualities are entities, such as 'number', 'weight', 'colour', 'energy', 'temperature', 'time', and so on. Other qualities may be described and formulated in more complex ways. In Egypt and elsewhere, protagonists of epistemic concepts are often shaped, and act, as gods. In gods, 'forces' experienced in interaction materialise. This applies both to various phenomena in nature – sun, water, wind – but also to forces at work in society, such as love, hate, and order.[20] While environmental phenomena may exist without human beings, and are only transformed into existence as an Other through appropriation, epistemes do not exist independently from humans and things. Mathematical epistemes such as a number, physical epistemes such as weight, phonetical epistemes such as a language, or theological epistemes such as a god do not exist other than as epistemic things.

The final purpose of producing epistemic things is to interact with those experiences that they represent or, more precisely, to manipulate them. The transformation of properties of a phenomenon into an epistemic thing is a fundamental means of appropriation and thus of manipulation, as the phenomenon is explained, or reduced, to its properties. Transformed into an episteme, the phenomenon is somehow predictable and may even be actively controlled: counted, weighed, expressed, adored, or damned.

Particularly concise are means of conceptualisation in which properties of things are identified by names and narratives. Egyptian gods, for example, can have names that are simply designations of phenomena, such as the sun god Aten (= sun disk), or a personification of the landscape (Figure 7). Other epistemic entities – such as the almost uncountable number of otherworldly Egyptian demons – bear names that tell whole little stories, so that to tell their name is to control them (Lucarelli, 2010). Such names and narratives form *mythemes*, that is, conceptual elements in which a particular experience has found a concise and familiar formulation within a paradigm of religiously grounded ontology (Goebs & Baines, 2018). Such mythemes act as epistemic things in that they are tools for producing further concepts. They can be arranged into stories – into *myths* – serving to explain, predict, and control. Each concise narrative opens up options and makes control possible (Figure 3).

5.2 Case Study: Choiak

An example of how epistemes are used is the description of the transformation of matter via mythemes of the Osirian narrative circle, as on the stela of Irtisen. Echoes of this Osirian mythology still appear in the epic stories of alchemy of

---

[20] As with others, terms such as 'episteme' and 'epistemic thing' are defined and used differently (Roßler, 2008). Epistemes may materialise quite differently: in purely immaterial ways, such as words, sounds, smell, colour, or glow (Goebs, 2007); in semi-material ways, such as concepts and ideas bound to 'media of erudition', like all the epistemes usually classified as scientific (El Hawary, 2018); and as hardware in the form of a fetish, image, or, again, as 'the script' itself (Nyord, 2020, 56–64). Even routines and practices such as dances, ceremonies, discourses, experiments, languages, and the wide field of 'intangible heritage' should be understood as epistemic things with which people interact, and vice versa: they interact with humans, inspire, and coerce, as any *thing* does (Rheinberger, 1997).

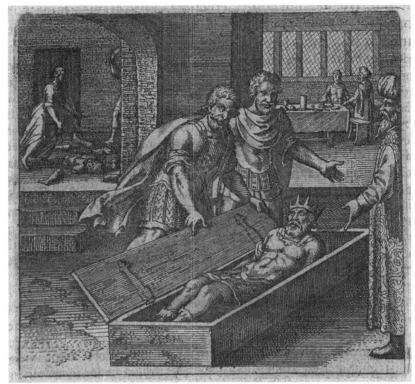

Quelle: Deutsche Fotothek

Figure 10 Illustration in the alchemical writing of Michael Maier (1617 / 1687). The old king (= the raw material) is dismembered (= broken down into its elementary components) and placed in a coffin (= oven) to be transformed by two harnessed 'forces' of nature into a new being, while a philosopher– alchemist controls the process.
Source: Public domain, via Wikimedia Commons, https://commons.wikimedia.org/wiki/ File:Fotothek_df_tg_0008203_Theosophie_%5E_Alchemie.jpg

early western modernity: the killing and dismemberment of the 'king' and his sealing in a coffin (Figure 10); the loss and recovery of shape; a post-mortem union with the female element; and, finally, the emergence of a 'young king'.[21] Irtisen's example also is interesting since, generally speaking, the mytheme, or god, Osiris has no relation to metallurgy. Osiris is no master of the forge or episteme of minerals. Narrative motifs constituting his myth rather reflect forces

---

[21] Fitzenreiter, 2020, 301–7. However, it is risky to deduce from such images that Pharaonic or Osirian epistemic concepts (= epistemic things) were being constantly hidden in use to explain matters of transfiguration. Rather it is possible to interpret their appearance in early modern literature as rediscoveries, reincorporated into alchemical epistemology. On connections between alchemy and Pharaonic culture see: Daumas, 1983; Richter, 2010; Ebeling, 2014.

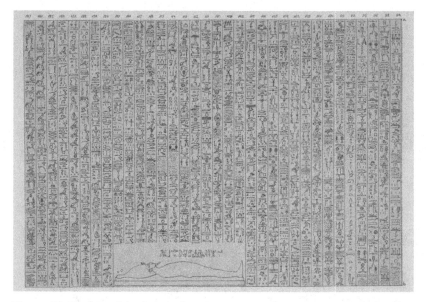

Figure 11 Section of the inscriptions in Room I of the northern roof chapel at Dendera with a depiction of 'the mould (*bed* / bd] of Chenti-Imentiju [of] one cubit in length' (Mariette, 1871: pl. 38).
Source: https://digi.ub.uni-heidelberg.de/diglit/mariette1873bd4/0044/image; Public Domain Mark 1.0.

of the social sphere: fratricide, spousal love and childcare, succession to office, inheritance, guilt, and punishment (Griffiths, 1970; Smith, 2017). Irtisen, however, is able to formulate the fundamental phenomenon of material transformation using the very same mythemes. This points to the universality of epistemes, once they are incorporated as appropriate means of explanation, prediction, and control within a collective worldview.

What could basically be interpreted as a somewhat frivolous play on mythemes in Irtisen's inscription – consider the burlesque battle depiction in his third confession – has found a much more serious and far more technical formulation on the walls of a chapel at Dendera. There, in the first century BCE, a compilation of texts has been eternalised, describing celebrations in the month of Choiak (Chassinat, 1966/8; Cauville, 1997a: 26–50; Cauville, 1997b: 14–28; Cauville, 1997c: 17–19) (Figure 11). Choiak in the Pharaonic calendar is counted as the fourth month of the inundation season, a period of receding Nile flood waters and reappearing fields, after which sowing starts. According to the Dendera inscription, this period was accompanied by the ritual manufacture of figurines. One figurine described in detail is that of a mummy with a human head, similar to the mummiform image of Osiris that was widespread

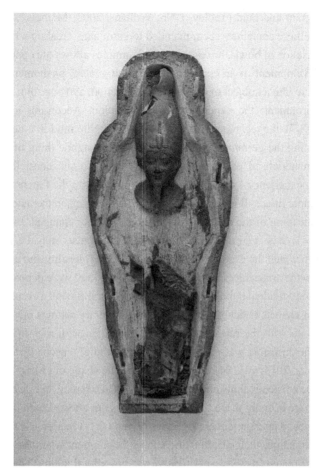

Figure 12 Coffin and fragment of a corn mummy with Osiris mask, c. 400–200 BCE (New York, Metropolitan Museum, Rogers Fund, 1958. Accession Number: 58.98a–d).
Source: https://collectionapi.metmuseum.org/api/collection/v1/iiif/570755/1357157/ main-image.

in the Middle Kingdom (Siffert, 2020). This figurine was made out of a mixture of 'barley with sand' (*it her shaj* / jt ḥr šꜥjj), first watered, then shaped in a mould, dried in the sun, and finally decorated and kept for one year.

Archaeological correlates are known: the so-called corn mummies, figurines made of mud and grain dating from the second half of the first millennium BCE (Raven, 1982; Centrone, 2009) (Figure 12). There are also archaeological precursors in the form of so-called Osiris beds or Osiris boxes from the New Kingdom, which are containers made in the silhouette of Osiris and filled with mud mixed with seeds. Even older are simple bowls from the Middle Kingdom containing grain and mud (Tooley, 1996; Willems, 2003; Michels, 2013). The seeds within these containers seem intended to germinate, creating a flowerbed.

This correlation of bowls, boxes, and corn mummies allows the opportunity to trace the development of an epistemic thing. The general phenomenon that is processed here into an object of explanation, prediction, and control is one of the natural environment: the experience of germination. According to Joachim F. Quack (2007), the technique of mixing seeds and Nile mud in a bowl has its origin in testing the germinability of seeds. As an epistemic thing of 'trial and error' – a materialised experimental practice or epistemic constellation that replicates an experience – the bowl made its way first into the funerary cult and then into temple rituals. It is worth remarking that, in taking on the outer shape of Osiris, the meaning of the epistemic thing most probably changed. Early attestation of bowls with germinated seeds in funerary spaces may be related to procedures in which the dead were involved in rituals of fertility and agriculture. According to the archaeological record, bowls of this kind were deposited not in connection to individual burials but during more general funerary events either in courtyards or chapels (Michels, 2013). Bowls in funerary settings may therefore have less to do with the resuscitation of the dead than with rites in which the support of the ancestors was called upon for agricultural reasons (Frazer, 1914: 158–200; Balz, 2014: 73–104). Transformed into the shape of Osiris in the New Kingdom, the epistemic thing changed its ontological function. While at funerary sites seeds were actually made to germinate, this is not attested with the finds of corn mummies. Apparently, these figurines do not (only) materialise the experience of germination, their manufacture enacts the moment when the landscape reappears and regains its shape and creative potency after flooding. The dissolved body of Osiris regains shape as a mummy, much the same way as the restructuring of melted metal is expressed by Irtisen. Thus, the ancient epistemic thing made out of soil and seeds in order to magically replicate and coerce the experience of germination, when shaped into the body of Osiris, became an epistemic tool of cyclical recovery of the whole of Egypt. While in the Dendera inscriptions the process of final germination out of this reshaped body is not detailed, it has found pictorial expression in a contemporary representation (Figure 13).

In addition to the manufacture of the corn mummy, inscriptions from Dendera describe a second figurine. This statuette was also outwardly designed as an image of the mummified Osiris, but was composed of different materials. The texts list a number of aromata and minerals, which in sum represent a kind of encyclopaedia of the Pharaonic mineral universe (Aufrère, 2007: 174–80). Book III records (translation after Chassinat, 1966/8: 380, 435):

'(§ 10:) What applies to these substances with a sweet smell, which are in the 'potent matter', they are twelve. To know the ingredients: Pine resin, cinnamon

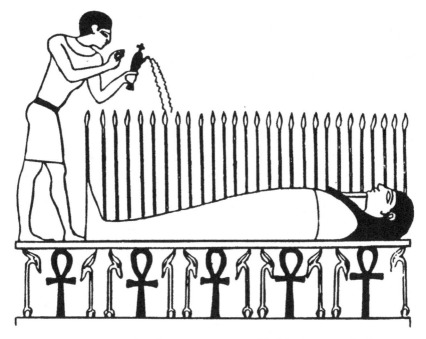

Figure 13 Plants sprouting from the mummy of Osiris; depiction in the temple of Philae (Budge, 1911).
Source: Public domain, via Wikimedia Commons, https://commons.wikimedia.org/wiki/File:Osiris_Philae.jpg.

[?], Cyprus grass from the oases, *gaijumaa* [?], sweet cane, rush from Ethiopia, juniper, sweet pine nuts, *fetetit* [?], *peqer* [?], mint, aspalate / rooibos [?]; total: twelve. Finely grind, pass through a cloth, add to the 'potent matter'.

(§ 11:) What applies to the genuine minerals found in the 'potent matter', there are fourteen [read: twenty-four] minerals. To know the constituents: silver, gold, genuine lapis lazuli, turquoise, raw turquoise [?], *seher* [?], *sherer* [?], carnelian, white flint, black flint, smoky crystal [?], rock crystal, amethyst, limestone, red jasper, copper vitriol, antimony, *senen* [?], haematite, *temechau* [?], true *techen* stone, green southern stone, green northern stone, *tiu* [?]; total: twenty-four. Ground all together, put into the 'potent matter''.

These substances were embedded in a mass called 'potent matter' (or raw material) (*qerehet shepes* / ḳrḥ.t šps). The mass was moulded into an 'egg' (*suhet* / swḥ.t), subjected to a kind of maturing process in a silver bowl, then shaped in a mould (which is associated with the god Sokar), before being dried and finally treated similarly to the corn mummy. Maarten Raven (1998) has been able to assign examples of Osiris figurines made out of clay to this object class. Direct precursors, such as the bowls containing grain and mud, are not known for this kind of figurine. However, a whole range of statuettes made of ceramic material or of wax / resin mixtures appear in funerary practices and in the field of defensive magic (Raven, 1983). Therefore, we might assume that the figurine from the Sokar model also represents the Osirian conversion of a much older epistemic concept and thing.

5.3 Religion As Technology

The dichotomy of the two figurines of Choiak sheds light on fundamental concepts of human–environment interaction in Pharaonic times. The corn mummy is closely related to techniques of agriculture. The preparation of soil, selection of grain, and watering of the basin imitate the preparation of fields for tilling at the end of the month of Choiak. Several aspects of the rite, therefore, may be understood along the lines of a ceremonial anticipation of agricultural techniques. This is in contrast to the second figurine, which embodies an image of an abiotic landscape that extends beyond the Nile Valley into the desert. As an epistemic thing this object is treated like the one representing the biotic world and brought into cyclical 'maturation' via a kind of alchemic recomposition within a 'primordial matter' (*qerehet* / ḳrḥ.t) endowed with 'potency' (*shepes* / šps). It remains open what sort of technical practices are imitated here. In any case, techniques of pottery production are in the background (mixing clay, maturing, etc.), as is also reflected in the fact that the ingredients are embedded in a matter designated as *qerehet* (ḳrḥ.t), which also means 'pottery' in the broadest sense (Raven, 1998; Fitzenreiter, 2021). Seen together, both objects reproduce experiences of a fundamental interaction with the universe: with the biotic environment in the form of germination, and with the abiotic environment in the form of mineral maturation, or material transformation.

However, as Émile Chassinat (1966/8: 23–52) emphatically points out, a purely functionalist interpretation of rites eternalised in the Dendera inscriptions as agrarian magic is too simplistic. Religious ritual is a practice in itself and it is done for its own sake, not primarily to secure a particular product. Corn mummies could possibly germinate, but they were not made to germinate because they were no longer samples to test germination. Beyond explaining farming and crafts, religious practice involves a broader issue in that it produces religion itself, an epistemic thing of its own kind, and one of the most valuable and important human goods – as well as one of the most fatal (Assmann, 2009). As an epistemic apparatus, religion has the purpose of constantly clarifying humanity's place in the world. This is achieved through a highly developed system of explanation, prediction, and control of the interaction between humans and the universe. A wide variety of techniques are developed and a wide variety of approaches are used to conceptualise this process technologically; or, as it should be called in this case, theologically. In the epistemic things of theology, the Other finds its final manifestation. In a certain way, within the epistemes of religion, a sometimes mysterious phenomenon meets its manifestation, which has been called 'the knowledge of things' in the introductory section. In case of the figurines, these phenomena are such inexplicable properties as the capacity for biotic substances to germinate and that of the transformation of non-biotic materials. Reformulated as epistemic things, such inherent capacities of matter are reflected, described, ordered, and systematised on an abstract level.[22] Understood this way, the mythemes of religious ontology and explicatory models of theology resemble the concepts of contemporary natural sciences.

But epistemic things of religion are much more than those of a scientific ontology, binarily fixed on true and untrue, can ever be. Surpassing scientific knowledge, epistemic things of religion are able to materialise exactly those capacities of the Other which are *not* understood, the 'knowledge of things' that remains hidden from humans and is sealed off from explanation, prediction, and control: the realms of the unknown, unpredictable, and dangerous, but also – of hope.

6 Technology and Society: Script

In previous sections, an emphasis was placed on the society of things and how they mean the world to humans. Nevertheless, whatever phenomena of a material or immaterial nature are involved, whether object or sensation, a thing is never a thing without humans. The same is true the other way round: people can never *be* without things, even in cases only involving people. So finally, the social side of things should be taken up once more, to consider how the interplay of things and humans configures the social, that is, the society of people (and things).[23]

Terms like technique and technology are traditionally applied to practices of interaction between humans and their non-human environment. However, many traits of this interaction can be observed in human-to-human relations as well. Such techniques are studied as cultural techniques (*Kulturtechniken*) in recent scholarship in the humanities (Kassung & Macho, 2013).[24] The interpretation of

---

[22] Examples of systematic reflection and ordering of these matters and their properties are documented in lists from temple libraries which arrange phenomena of the natural and cultural environment (landscape, plants, animals, minerals, settlements, temples, fetishes, etc.) into categories of 'divine' power. For this, see von Lieven, 2004.

[23] On 'Social No. 1' as the society of people and 'Social No. 2' as the society of people and things, see Latour, 2005.

[24] On differences and commonalities between Cultural Studies and *Kulturtechnikwissenschaften*, see Geoghegan, 2013. See also Fitzenreiter, 2020: 46–73.

cultural practice as cultural techniques makes cultural studies a special branch within the wider field of technology. Developed to study cultural media in the broadest sense, the terminological tools and methodological approaches of cultural studies are particularly useful in interpreting a special body of evidence that shapes Pharaonic culture in a peculiar way: script (Baines, 2007).

6.1 Culture, Society, and Writing

In terms of the legacies of Pharaonic material culture, the most striking feature today is not diet – that Egyptians were bread eaters and beer drinkers – but writing. Hieroglyphs define Pharaonic culture, or the totality of features that give 'the Pharaonic' its quality as an episteme.[25] Pharaonic culture begins in the late fourth millennium BCE, at the time that an inventory of specific pictorial signs appears, first as proto-script in the middle of the fourth millennium BCE (Morenz, 2004), and finally as a fully developed writing system during the First to Third Dynasties (c. 3000 to 2500 BCE) (Kahl, 1994). Pharaonic culture ends with its 'last inscription' in the temple of Philae in 394 CE (Parkinson, 2005: 19). Even the Egyptian language does not have this qualifying effect. The culture of the Coptic period that followed, which used an alphabetic script based on Greek letters to write the same Egyptian language, is treated as an epistemic thing in its own right.

The artificial separation of 'Pharaonic' from 'Coptic' culture, and the latter again from 'Arab' and 'Islamic' cultures, demonstrates that 'culture' as an episteme is not unproblematic. As appropriate as it is to question the term 'culture' in its normative use, however, it remains the case that commonalities *and* differences play their roles in ordering remnants of the past. Archaeological cultures as such are primarily typological inventories, synthesising phenomena which share common characteristics and qualifying people who are entangled with and 'assembled' by these phenomena (see Section 3). When looking at cultural expressions, however, it is equally important to grasp characteristic differences. As Ferdinand de Saussure (1959: 121–2) notes: only difference makes meaning.[26] It is exactly those small but significant differences – the

---

[25] I prefer to speak of 'Pharaonic' rather than 'ancient Egyptian' in relation to culture, as the latter inadmissibly ignores all other pre-modern ('ancient') cultural epochs of Egypt, both those of the pre-Pharaonic period and – especially – those of Late Antiquity, the Middle Ages, and the early modern period. On whether these epoch designations which originate from western evolutionary concepts are at all applicable to the East Mediterranean region, or rather not, see Bauer, 2018. Further, to speak of the 'Pharaonic' allows us to characterise related phenomena which are not confined to the geographical space of Egypt proper and to the temporal frame of antiquity. The 'Pharaonic' is a legacy that persists beyond 'ancient Egypt'.

[26] The phenomenon of generating meaning through differences is discussed in detail by Derrida (1997), who coins the concept of *différance*, using the example of the relationship between

phonemes of culture(s) – that arouse the interest of cultural studies. Bread and beer may unite, or may divide, or may create a space of mutual (mis-) understanding. To look for evidence as remnants of cultural technique loosens the straitjacket of typology and gets to the core of cultural entanglement or, as sketched in Section 3, of how people create themselves as cultural entities by producing difference. Therefore, to interpret culture as an arena of cultural technique means to look for what else happens during technical interaction, sometimes deliberately but often incidentally, in a way that can be unexpected and even hidden from the actors: the creation of society and its specific, as well as fluid, cultural traits.

Previous sections dealt with the fact that as things are used, they make people what they are. The reference to practice is important. It is not things that make people, but their use: interaction and resulting interconnectedness (Hahn, 2019). But practices not only make humans people, they also subject them to the network of things. If a certain level of cultural entanglement with things is reached, people are dependent on 'cultural achievements'. They cannot go back without losing much of their acquired personhood, their social and cultural identity, and in some cases even their means of physical self-preservation (Hodder, 2012: 179–205). Within such a network of dependencies and entanglements, society emerges as an epistemic thing, as an embodiment or reification (*Verdinglichung*) of these relations (Honneth, 2015). As such, society is knitted anew in each moment of interaction, but persists as an epistemic thing of its own kind.

Besides general human–environment interaction, communication and cooperation between humans is just one of the many networks of interaction that constitute society. But it is one which shapes its very appearance, as well as its cultural remnants, in a particular way. Human communication practices specific cultural techniques and uses particular tools to do so. The 'weapon of war' may be interpreted as one of the first instruments to serve solely as a tool to interfere in social relations. As an oversized knife or modified axe, it originates from tools of human–environment interactions, from activities of herding and hunting. As weapons, these precursors attained a new and specific appearance that was suitable for hunting and herding humans, and new terminology (e.g., 'sword' or 'mace') that addressed this purpose. Professional use of weapons – techniques of so-called honourable fighting – creates a difference between the hunt and warfare, making the enemy a victim, not prey. The weapon serves the social.

---

writing and language which will be discussed below. A difference between *différence* and *différance* is only visible in script, not audible in speech.

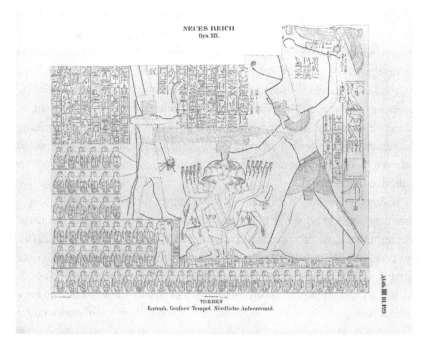

Figure 14 Warfare and writing as social engineering. King Seti I smiting a 'bird of ten' out of enemies in front of the god Amun, who is pulling a row of personifications inscribed with the designations of foreign regions, towns, and people. Decoration of the outer walls of the great Amun temple at Karnak, c. 1300 BCE.

Source: Lepsius, 1849–59: vol. III, pl. 129. www.edoc3.bibliothek.uni-halle.de/lepsius/page/abt3/band6/image/03061290.jpg.

While a weapon may act quite directly, many cultural techniques and their instruments share the peculiarity of working indirectly, or symbolically. They prefer to interfere with the materiality of epistemic things, to transform the web of meaning. Even the proper purpose of a weapon is not necessarily to kill but to demonstrate the potency to kill, through display and posture. Transforming the practical potency of killing into symbolic potency, the weapon becomes a symbol of its function (Figure 14). Comparably, symbolic potency is inherent in a sceptre, a wand, a cult object, or an amulet. Symbolic devices accompany and potentiate techniques of human interaction on all levels of social activity, being insignia handed over in the transfer of social positions, amulets for healing treatments, and even units of accounting in economic transactions, so that to a considerable extent cultural techniques are symbolic and their tools are symbols.

Probably the most important instrument in this sense, next to the weapon or, nowadays, money, is script (Grube, Kogge, & Krämer, 2005). In script, symbolic, or epistemic, things materialise and are bound to a medium. In particular, a 'text' of what is told or thought meets it materialisation in script, the same way as 'images' of what is seen or imagined are materialised in icons.[27] Even non-glottic and non-visual experiences may manifest themselves in script, such as tacit knowledge recorded in dance steps, knitting patterns, and tablatures. Sound (musical notation), feelings (emoticons), and other phenomena are also recordable in script (Harris, 1995).

In contrast to a widespread misconception which claims a special relationship between script and language, materialising speech by means of script is usually only a deviation of an effort to materialise text and is hardly the task of script itself.[28] The inherent logocentrism of common conceptions of writing, however, has resulted in an assumption that script is just a carrier of spoken language. This overlooks the fact that script is a highly complex medium in itself. Hardly any other achievement of antiquity has left comparable imprint on the cultural superstructure of human society. Script, not language, is the tool that makes the Aristotelian separation of skill and knowledge possible, a separation which is replicated in the distinction between science (= applied research) and humanities (= research without application). In historical research, too, use of script, not of language, is considered a turning point between pre-history and history. The dichotomy of non-script versus script, or literate and illiterate, shapes the epistemological paradigm of the post-antique world in that religion, morality, civilisation, culture, and so on are measured by script (Pinarello, 2015: 20).[29] Even the ontological impact of script, and its derivatives, on humans themselves can hardly be underestimated: to interact with script makes people different and even makes them different people.[30] To interact with script is one of the most characteristic operations unique to humankind, marking its ultimate difference

---

[27] On the distinction of *text* and *image* from their materialisations in a *script* or an *icon*, see Morenz & Schorsch, 2007.

[28] At least outside of linguistic studies, when using script to record the spoken. For early attempts to record actual intonation (= speech) via musical notation, see Crystal, 2010: 170. Nowadays, special characters are used in linguistics to transcribe phonetic phenomena (www.international-phoneticassociation.org, accessed 15 July 2021). All other scripts in use are more or less a mixture of glottal and non-glottal elements; for this, see Harris, 1995.

[29] Script controls the ontological foundations of all schools of thought (western as eastern as well) which create strict divisions between concept and experience. Script seduces people into thinking that epistemes are more real than experience (which they are produced by). It is only in the age of 'turns' that these dichotomies are being abolished and that it is being made clear that meaning does not precede its sign (Derrida, 1997).

[30] While cyborgs consisting of man and machine (Haraway, 1991) or the takeover of humanity by artificial intelligence (https://manifesto.ai, accessed 4 June 2021) are currently the topics of excited debate, scripts have produced completely new people/hybrids for about 5,000 years: first of all the writer and the reader (Morenz, 1996) and later on all the inhabitants of the 'Gutenberg galaxy' of modernity (McLuhan, 1962).

to any other species (so far). It is not for nothing that, next to the weapon, the pen is the essential symbol of law, order, and any other central societal phenomena.

6.2 Hieroglyphs

Hieroglyphs have their own particular symbolic capacity, being icons of Pharaonic culture par excellence. Probably because of this, techniques of writing and reading have received greater interest in Egyptological research than other techniques, such as food or pottery production. As far as entanglement goes, because hieroglyphs are the symbol of the Pharaonic, an Egyptologist is therefore someone capable of interacting with hieroglyphs. Nonetheless, writing and reading as techniques, and script as an epistemic thing, have remained somewhat neglected in Egyptological research. Traditionally, an emphasis has been placed on language, its vocabulary, and its grammar (Allen, 2014: 455–62), thus foregrounding script as a depiction of speech (Allen, 2013). But script is much more than language and hieroglyphs are a striking example of this.

Obviously, the relationship of script and language is of utmost importance for understanding a visual language script, but from a technological perspective, writing simply means the use of scribal techniques to materialise and subsequently decode meaning – and not speech[31] – via reference to a pictorial sign. In the case of a *picture script*, the reference between a pictorial sign, or *icon*, and meaning is established directly without a diversion via phonation. In the case of a *visual language script*, there is a two-step process. As a first step, a sound has to be referenced by a written sign (*grapheme*). In a second step, this sound, or a sequence of sounds, has to be referenced to a meaning, and here the sound materialises in the speech of a spoken language (Saussure, 1959: 44). Ideally, the sign (the grapheme) has no relation itself to meaning.[32]

It is not necessary to view double referencing as a sole criterion for 'real' script (Baines, 2007: 3–30; Morenz, 2021), for even in contemporary visual language scripts elements of referencing via pictorial signs frequently remain.[33]

---

[31] There are magical spells where the exact pronunciation may be part of the record, even without an apparent meaning, as in 'abracadabra'.

[32] It should be noted that a spoken language referred to in a script is usually not just materialised everyday speech, but a high-level *visual* language with its own grammatical rules and vocabulary. It is a phenomenon of appropriation if patterns and vocabulary of formalised and artificial visual language are also adapted (to a certain degree) in everyday speech and its spoken language, as in most western or high-register (school) languages or in modern standard Arabic (*al-fuṣḥā*; الْفُصْحَى).

[33] It is common practice in alphabetic scripts today to use pictorial signs like punctuation marks, and so on. For multimodality in Pharaonic script in general, see Kammerzell, 2021. We should also note that with cursive visual languages such as Demotic reading often means visual pattern recognition and not phonetic referencing.

Double-referenced visual language actually prevailed in Pharaonic Egypt, though the number of pictorial signs in the writing systems is relatively high. But the special, exciting, and in a way essential feature of hieroglyphs is not that they mostly produce meaning via reference to sound, but that this meaning is not infrequently produced via reference to pictures (Assmann & Assmann, 2003). This reference could be the meaning of the icon itself, but could also be a derivation related to the image's phonation. The latter occurs in *rebus* script (Morenz, 2004), a strictly pictorial technique that was crucial to the development of the Pharaonic writing system as it linked a sign referencing a specific meaning by the picture shown to a sound with similar phonetic features. Thus, a rebus makes, out of a specific visual reference, an archetypal phonetic one. In early modern (western) appropriation of hieroglyphics this aspect was of particular importance, and in fact still is (Mauelshagen, 2007).

Egyptologists' interest in script as an independent medium is constantly growing. The traditional focus on the emergence of the writing system itself, or on how meaning and signs are correlated (Graff & Jimenez Serrano, 2015), is being extended by an interest in special or pseudo-scripts that escape the primacy of referencing with speech (Van der Moezel, 2016; Haring, 2018), as well as in cryptography, enigmatic scripts, and script games in which techniques of referencing are haphazardly mixed (Drioton & Fairman, 1992; Darnell, 2004; Morenz, 2008; Klotz & Stauder, 2020). Ptolemaic studies analyse script that operates not only at the level of signs but also by correlating text with its architectural setting under the heading of 'temple grammar' (*grammaire du temple*) (Arpagaus, 2021). Studies on techniques of interaction with script deal with modes of writing and reading, of knowledge formation and knowledge acquisition, and with the literary field in general (Morenz, 1996; Parkinson, 2002; Quirke, 2004; Baines, 2007; Rashwan, 2019; Morenz, 2020). Most recently, the 'material turn' is stimulating research on writing proper, such as penning techniques, individual writing styles, and the like (Piquette, 2018; Ragazzoli, 2019; Regulski, 2020a; Carlig et al., 2020; Davies & Laboury, 2020). Increasingly, writing is being recognised as a form of practice and script no longer rated as just a vehicle for language or textual meaning, but as a product and an epistemic thing of its own kind (Pinarello, 2015).

6.3 Case Study: The Rosetta Stone

6.3.1 A Monument to Script

An iconic monument of script and script research, in Egyptology and beyond, is the so-called Rosetta Stone: a stela of black granite, once over two metres high, of which the lower 118 cm has been preserved (Figure 15) (Quirke & Andrews,

Figure 15 The Rosetta Stone, found at Rashid, probably from the temple of Sais
or Memphis, c. 196 BCE(London, BM EA 24).
Source: © Hans Hillewaert, licensed under the Creative Commons Attribution-Share Alike
4.0 International license, https://commons.wikimedia.org/wiki/File:Rosetta_Stone.JPG; ©
Hans Hillewaert.

1988).[34] Found at Rashid (Rosetta) in 1799, it possibly originates from the
temples of Sais or Memphis. Although not the only such monument, it owes its
veritable pop status to the role its inscription played in deciphering Pharaonic
visual language as well as to its object biography: initially because of its status
as a colonial trophy in the competition between France and England to decipher
hieroglyphs, and nowadays because of its postcolonial charging as a monument
of divergent national and cultural self-perceptions (Valbelle & Leclant, 1999;
Parkinson, 2005; Ray, 2008; Downs, 2020; Buchwald & Greco Josefowicz,
2020). As a monument that 'assembles' people on many levels, at many times,
and in many places, it is a fitting example of the complexity of cultural and social
networks that emerge out of techniques and things, revolving around script.

The creation of the stela goes back to a decree issued by King Ptolemy
V in year nine of his reign (196 BCE) on the occasion of a council of priests

---

[34] http://rosettastone.hieroglyphic-texts.net (accessed 9 June 2021); https://rosetta-stone.dh.uni-
leipzig.de/rs/ (accessed 9 June 2021).

of Egyptian temples in Memphis. According to circumstances indicated in the text, this meeting was brought about by a wave of revolts against the Ptolemaic dynasty which necessitated a realignment in the relationship between the Ptolemaic regime and the temples. The text itself appears in three different scriptorial versions. The upper version is written in hieroglyphs, the middle one in Demotic cursive, and the last one in Greek alphabetic characters, each referencing its respective visual language: Ancient Egyptian (*égyptien de tradition*) (Vernus, 2017), Demotic, and Greek.

The text materialised in each version is more or less the same and is composed of four sections (Hoffmann & Pfeiffer, 2021). An introduction gives an elaborate titulature of the king and the date, followed by a description of the occasion and the locality of the assembly. The second section retells a fictitious speech by the assembled priesthood which details favours that were granted by the king and the royal house to temples and their staff; recalls homeland defence strategies and counterinsurgency; and stresses that an amnesty was proclaimed that included debt relief to temples. Finally, benefits for sacred animals and royal involvement in temple construction are highlighted. In response, the transition to the third section proclaims that, in return, the king and his house were favoured by the gods and bestowed with rulership. To make this manifest, it is stipulated that the cult of the royal family shall be expanded by installing a cult image of the king in the company of the local god in each temple, as well as by manufacturing a second, processional image and its shrine. Two festival days per month and a five-day festival in the first month of inundation season are scheduled for the cult of the king's statue, and it is noted that the king's cult may also be performed in private shrines. The inscription closes with a formula ordering that this very text was to be recorded in all relevant temples by inscriptions in the three visual languages mentioned.

The custom of displaying monuments inscribed in multiple scripts is attested several times under the Ptolemies (Bowman et al., 2021). Numerous versions are preserved of a decree issued under Ptolemy III (Figure 16) (Pfeiffer, 2004), and in addition to the Rosetta Stone there are others of Ptolemy V (Hoffmann & Pfeiffer, 2021: 26–44). A final example of this custom is a stela commissioned by the first Roman prefect, C. Cornelius Gallus from Philae, the inscription of which is written in hieroglyphs, Latin, and Greek, symbolically putting an end to the tradition of Ptolemaic trilingues (Hoffmann, Minas-Nerpel, & Pfeiffer, 2009).

Even though there are echoes of older monuments in the text of the Rosetta Stone and similar inscriptions, these were nonetheless relatively new monuments in type and design. Multilingual inscribed stelae were not customary

Figure 16: Canopus decree of Ptolemaios III, found at Kom el-Hisn, c. 238
BCE (Cairo, CG 22186).
Source: montage by the author after Kamal, 1904: Pl. LIX, LX, LXI.

among the pharaohs, although they were well known in the multi-ethnic and multi-cultural Persian Empire (Briant, 1999). The Persian administrative structure, developed along ethnic and cultural divisions, had been adopted by the polities of the Diadochi and thus by the Ptolemies (Thompson, 2018). The decisive role script played in engineering such a social constellation of 'unity in diversity' is reflected in the complex practical networks generated around the monument.

6.3.2 Materiality

During the making of the stela, the role of script was to materialise a decree. Through the act of being written, in this case on a stela of black stone, the decree, which had previously been a will negotiated between people, became manifest. This central function of script as a tool to create epistemic things can be postulated for practically all script, including its earliest forms. By materialisation in script, meaning is referenced, and this meaning is usually understood as a *text*. That is why so often no distinction is made between *inscription* and *text* at all: an inscription like that of the Rosetta Stone, seen as an epistemic thing, *is* meaning, as text, made manifest. To generate the (pictorial) presence of meaning is a first criterion for script in the broadest sense.

The Rosetta Stone uses three different scripts and thus, in addition to a rather abstract meaning more or less identical in all three texts, gives materiality to three quite distinct visual languages. This had enormous consequences for its function as a vehicle of decipherment much later, but was originally configured quite differently. The three versions did not serve to complement each other in establishing a meaning that was shared (as in the struggle for decipherment), but addressed and defined segments of society that were different. At the same time, by marking differences, these segments acquired a culturally tangible imprint. These important little differences are not expressed by different texts, but find their visible expression in different characters, addressing different forms of (technical) encoding meaning, as well as of writing. This is even made explicit in the final section of the inscription, where the hieroglyphic version refers to hieroglyphs as 'script of divine words' (*sesh en medu-netjer* / sš n mdw-nṯr), identifies Demotic script as 'script of documents' (*sesh en shaj* / sš n šꜥy), and marks Greek script as 'letters of the Greeks' (*sekhaj en hau-nebu* /sḫꜣy n ḥꜣw-nbw). In the hieroglyphic writing, the phrase 'script of documents' in reference to Demotic and the term 'letter' (of the Greeks) are accompanied by the icon for 'tongue' (⊓ / F 20), indicating speech, whereas this icon is missing in the classification of hieroglyphic writing. At the same time, the two Egyptian scripts are distinguished by the designation 'iconographic script', as marked by the sign for the scribe's/painter's palette (⌂/ Y 3), from the 'letters' of the Greeks, to which only the 'tongue' is assigned.[35] In this way, it is made explicit that each section is made for a different type of encoding and decoding technique.

In demanding different ways of decoding and encoding meaning, the inscription makes different writers and readers, in somewhat the same way as different people are made by distinct forms of food production and consumption. Embedded in the distinctive social and cultural context of Ptolemaic Egypt, where different cultural techniques of writing and reading were used by different members of society, the Rosetta Stone's inscription is an interesting example of how these differences have been recognised, conceptualised, and addressed. Script and speech, as media of the production of socio-cultural similarities and differences, are thematised in the monument itself. This indicates that such differences and similarities were recognised as being important defining elements in social relations. Further, and this is maybe the most important hint of the role things play while establishing society, these differences and similarities are not *a priori*, but depend on specific media of expression. In this case, these media are different scribal signs demanding different techniques of writing and reading, thus creating small differences even while referencing an identical text. This brings about a reification of the specific ambiguity of a multi-ethnic society: 'Greekness' is expressed by writing and reading Greek characters, but not necessarily by being Greek. And there are no 'Egyptians', but people reading either hieroglyphs or Demotic, or even both, or even all three scripts.[36]

6.3.3 Performance

By encoding meaning in script, meaning is given enduring materiality and, in turn, reality and agency. This process enables an (apparent) de-temporalisation and de-spatialisation of meaning ('apparent' because every realisation of meaning is nevertheless bound to its presence in time and space) as well as its detachment from its producers. Epistemes captured in script thus become actants of their own particular quality. As such, scripts are action-guiding or stimulating, or even action-triggering and enforcing. This is precisely the sense of the decree beyond its textual message. The threefold script-based

---

[35] The Demotic text is less scrupulous and consistently speaks of 'script' (*sekh* / sḫ); the Greek text writes that the inscription should be written by 'sacred' (*hierois* / ΙΕΡΟΙΣ), 'native' (*enchoriois* / ΕΓΧΩΡΙΟΙΣ) and 'Greek' (*hellenikois* / ΕΛΛΗΝΙΚΟΙΣ) 'characters' (*grammasin* / ΓΡΑΜΜ {Λ}[Α]ΣΙΝ). This is a nice example of how pictorial writing may be much more precise than other variants of script.

[36] It is only the Roman C. Cornelius Gallus who divides the readers in 'latiners', 'greekers', and 'hieroglyphers'.

manifestation of the same text is intended to set and to enforce in a symbolic, quasi-magical way what is written down. To transform the process of decision-making among people at a council into script means to detach it from the actors, to constitute it as an epistemic thing, and to let it out again as an actant. It urges people to manufacture cult images, instigate festivals, and practice accordingly. We might therefore postulate that a second general criterion for what script *is*, is to make meaning performative (Roeder, 2003).

Given this, it is surprisingly how often the precise meaning of text remains opaque and ambiguous. Meaning may depend not only on the written words or symbols, but on the material properties of the writing material, the use of particular signs, or scribal idiosyncrasies. In short, a document as a whole can mean much more than its text expresses (Morenz, 2008; Quack & Luft, 2021). In the case of the Rosetta Stone, this is made obvious by the manifestation of a single text in three versions in three visual languages. Without even reading, but just by observation, differences appear that make sense independently of the text. The monument leaves a first impression that it is not the text but the appearance of triple writing that constitutes the special, and perhaps even overriding, meaning of the monument as reification of a vision of Ptolemaic society.

The idea that the meaning of a text and the meaning of its materialisation are two different aspects has been studied as a particular property of media by Marshall McLuhan (1964). According to McLuhan, the (narrower) meaning of a text as *content* should be distinguished from the actual meaning of the document as its *essence*. This essence results, for example, from the way it is materialised: 'the medium is the message'. In the case of the Rosetta Stone, the black materiality of the stela, the three variants of writing and probably a number of other features constituted the essence of the medium, while the inscriptions conserve the narrower content, and could probably hope for a fairly limited interested readership. Nowadays, only a small group of specialists interacts with this content, but the stela is prized for its essence as a testimony to the visual languages of Pharaonic times. Even its former essence as a monument of norm-setting and safeguarding of intersocial and intercultural dynamics fades into the background.

It would seem that while the materiality and content of an inscription tend to be unchanging, within the context of appropriation essence, and thus agency, are more changeable. To comprehend, or interact, with script means to activate its potential to produce meaning on the one hand, and to realise this potential on the other: two aspects that can clearly diverge. Although the meaning of the content of the three texts written on the Rosetta Stone is supposed to be approximately the same, each has the potential to prompt different interpretations. This starts at a simple technical level in that reading hieroglyphs or Greek letters requires completely different techniques of interaction with signs. Moreover, as is the case today, few recipients will have mastered all three scripts in such a way that they were able to fully comprehend all of the texts and their contents. Some of the sections will have served as visually browsed graphics, while others served to generate meaning by being read, in full or partially. Since the process of registering meaning does not necessarily involve reading, the actual sense and, in turn, outcome of the agency of a script may be something completely different from the intention of those who produced it; for example, not to deify Ptolemy V and to pacify Egypt but to serve the decipherment of hieroglyphs.

Such striking ambiguities demonstrate that properties such as agency, when applied to a thing, are framed during interaction by the conceptual pair of potential *performance* – what effect or meaning the thing can produce – and realised *emergence*: what effect or meaning it actually produces (Austin, 1962; Fischer-Lichte, 2005; Fitzenreiter, 2015). For any possible performance, *presence* is the prerequisite (Frese, Hornbacher, & Willer, 2015), where presence means not only being in itself, but interacting. If it had not been installed in front of a temple in Ptolemaic times and recognised by people, even if just a few, the Rosetta Stone would have remained just a block of black stone. Similarly, without its removal by French officer Pierre Bouchard, it would have remained, at least for the time being, a block of building material reused within the Rosetta fortification. The performative potential of a block of building material only became manifest when the scratches on its surface were recognised as an inscription. The process of transforming simple existence into performative presence is thus additionally bound to certain competencies, and to its framing paradigm. Bouchard was able to recognise on this object Greek characters and their special relationship to hieroglyphs, while the French invaders of Egypt, seen as a cultural collective, viewed themselves to be not only on a conquering expedition of the present but on a campaign to appropriate the past. It is only within this paradigm that the stone became valuable and a sought-after item of booty, not only to the French but the British too. Paradigm therefore is to the emergence of a thing what presence is to its performance. Just as an object has to be experienceable to be able to interact with people as a thing, people are only able to interact with things according to their skill and conceptual frameworks. Sometimes, in ANT and similar approaches, the agency of objects may be overstressed, but it is important to note that agency or affordance are by no means abilities which are inherent to a given object. They are caused and they are framed by practical networks of interaction. Agency (of objects) describes a relation, rather than a property, and this is why an object only becomes a thing by interaction.

6.3.4 Transformation

Interaction with script is often paradoxical in that, to be an epistemic thing, the inscription only needs writers but no readers. To understand the essence of an inscription, sometimes there is no need to read it. Bouchard, though he was unable to grasp the meaning of the text of the inscription, immediately understood the meaning, or importance, of the find,[37] which was not that of the content of the text itself and not even the essence of the stela in Ptolemaic times. All of this leads to a final aspect of the interaction with things: that anything can be reworked by secondary interaction in such a way that it becomes a new kind of thing. The process has been described by Krzysztof Pomian (1984) as one in which an object becomes a 'semiophor', or carrier of some kind of meaning that was not originally inherent to it or intended. The performance of this meaning is neither predictable nor logical and often, in fact, surreal. This is particularly true in the case of holy scriptures, but applies also to laws, *belles lettres*, and works of art in general. And it happens to practically all objects that become the focus of archaeology as finds and findings, when their content remains more or less untouched but their essence changes totally: from bread or pot to museum piece.

Today, the essence of the Rosetta Stone is, above all, as a monument to Egyptology, never understood by 99% of museum visitors in its textual content but very well understood by practically all of them in its cultural essence. Since its discovery, and as framed by shifting paradigms, the stone has been charged with secondary epistemic values. The resulting agency incites struggles for intellectual and moral interpretative dominance, including authority over its materiality, with the question of to whom and where does the thing 'belong'? (Colla, 2007: 76; Ray, 2008: 145–63; Downs, 2020: 210–15; Regulski, 2020b: 224–7; Abd El Gawad, 2022). That the very claim of ownership gets such attention places a spotlight on how close the relationship between things and people may be. To be the possessor and rightful owner of a thing is the final proof of hybridisation. To claim heritage means to proclaim identity out of physical entanglement. This holds particularly true in situations when, as in the case of the Rosetta Stone, relations of political dependence and cultural determination are negotiated. Certain objects become symbols or reifications of strained relations. The Rosetta Stone is an example of how, propelled by the actor–networks circling around it, one particular example in a group of similar objects becomes an icon, while its brothers and sisters – like the better preserved

---

[37] In German there is one word that covers both 'meaning' and 'importance': *Bedeutung*.

stela with the Canopus decree from Kom el-Hisn – gather dust more or less unnoticed (Figure 16).

6.4 Time

To become such a semiophor of cultural appropriation, the potential of things to transgress human timescapes is of utmost importance. As mentioned above, quite abstract meanings can become eternalised by being materialised in script. It is the same as when people eternalise themselves through things, as Ptolemy V wanted to do by establishing his statues in every temple. But people may also be eternalised unintentionally by things that they have become entangled with. Tools and other media are not only 'extensions of man' in the sense of improving capacity for material production, they are also extensions of people in an ontological sense. If material elements of personality last – be it tools, books, or even dead bodies – aspects of individuality transgress time. Reading a book, we sit together with great thinkers of antiquity (Assmann, 2018: 203), and so do collectives as they transform their social relations into entities and things – material or epistemic foundations – that defy natural processes of dissolution, such as religion, law, and culture. Being media apparently suspended of time (and space), things become traces and messages of the people they were once entangled with and afford entanglement for generations to come. Through this process, *cultural memory* as an epistemic thing is created again and again (Assmann, 1992).

The fundamental agency of script – and its third fundamental property – lies in its ability to entangle people, even across generations. Epistemes, captured in script, form a reservoir of conceptual tools that people make use of in the construction of identity. A monument such as the Rosetta Stone 'assembles' people over millennia. To evoke a kind of cultural memory was already its function when it was manufactured in the time of the Ptolemies, using not only the contemporary scripts of Demotic and Greek, but time-honoured hieroglyphs as well. The stela, which was probably adorned with the depiction of the king in front of Egypt's divinities (Hoffmann & Pfeiffer, 2021: 39, Abb. 5), visually expressed the idea of cultural depth. Along with affirming the notion of unrelenting Pharaonic power, it outlined the multi-social Ptolemaic present in passages written in Demotic and Greek. In its text, ostensibly traditional motifs, such as benefactions of the king and the reciprocal affection of the gods (Assmann, 1990), are combined with novel aspects originating from a Macedonian cult of heroes and of the royal family (Minas-Nerpel, 2019). In a situation of political instability, such *invention of tradition* (Hobsbawm & Ranger, 1983) out of epistemes and things from the reservoir of cultural memory was intended to reaffirm Ptolemaic rule by allusion to past times of glory, both of Pharaonic Egypt and Macedonia.

This interplay of tradition and innovation, of past and present, points to the occurrence of 'the Pharaonic' as a cultural form or pattern existing beyond 'bread [and] beer' and Ptolemaic politics. Being an episteme of cultural memory, 'the Pharaonic' displays extraordinary agency in emancipating itself from time and space, from antiquity, and also from the Nile Valley. Pharaonic things, such as hieroglyphs, pictures, costumes, pyramids, obelisks, sphinxes, and mummies, have been and continue to be reshaped into new kinds of semiophors and integrated into contexts in which they acquire new agency and generate new fascination (Fitzenreiter, 2018). Keywords such as *Egyptomania, Egyptian revival*, or *fara'uniya* (فرعونية) are witness to the potential ongoing agency of Pharaonic culture (Colla, 2007: 273–7; Reid, 2015; El Hawary, 2015; Versluys, 2020). Pharaonic culture assembled people in the past and continues to do so today (Figure 17). Things exist within a dilated time structure, different from that of humans, and while human perception is bound to a specific, biologically determined timescape, it is by things that this timescape may be transgressed. Things transcend human perception and it is by interacting with things that people are able to experience and engage with phenomena that are beyond their own timescapes.

7 Conclusion

The aim of the approach presented here has been to contribute to recent shifts within Egyptology away from histories of techniques in a narrower sense – of 'pots without people' – towards a history of technology that interprets techniques as relations within a culture derived from 'pots entangled to people'. In a methodological sense, the example of script discussed in the last section may be particularly helpful. Techniques of writing may seem to be quite complex arenas of human interaction, but in fact they are by no means unusual, and in a way quite simple. Terminology that is useful for dealing with script-based culture may be applied in more or less the same way to any evidence available to archaeology. Dimensions of tangible and intangible materialisation, of the shifting *différance* (Derrida, 1997) between content and essence, of the tension between performative properties and actual emergence, and, finally, the ambiguous status of things, applies to any interaction between humans and the wider environment. The baking of a bread roll initiates a process of tangible materialisation of an object and, at the same time, of its intangible dimension, the same way as writing down a text produces a tangible inscription and, jointly, an intangible meaning. Baking produces the loaf as a singular *object* and 'bread'

(a)

(b)

Figure 17 It comes to life – Pharaonic epistemes as actants around 1920–30.
a) Mahmoud Mokhtar: Nahdet Masr (نهضة مصر / Resurrection of Egypt), an iconic example of *fara'uniya*; Granit, 1920/21, Cairo. Source: Photo by FORTEPAN / Inkey Tibor, public domain, via Wikimedia Commons, https://commons.wikimedia.org/w/index.php?curid=51282609
b) Official film poster for The Mummy (1932)
Source: Public domain, via Wikimedia Commons, https://commons.wikimedia.org/wiki/File:The_Mummy_1932_film_poster.jpg.

as an abstract *episteme*. In its double substance as *content* (i.e., carbohydrate supplier) and *essence* (i.e., means of individual, social, and cultural identity and reproduction), bread circulates in a network in which it possesses certain properties, or *agency*, particularly of course to people who are hungry. The way in which its properties are enabled, so that it becomes a *performant* able to trigger certain effects, is framed by its *presence*, meaning simply access to bread in general. On the other hand, actual reception and *emergence* – what is experienced – is tied to particular networks of knowledge and *paradigm*. What satiates one person may arouse disgust in another, a well-known effect of so-called local delicacies, not to mention the secondary elaboration into a *semiophor*, making the innocent bun an offering, sacramental host, item of intangible heritage, or museum piece.

To study culture from the point of view of technology is to interpret culture as the constant interaction and resulting entanglement of things and humans. This helps to overcome problematic divisions that are often implied between skill and knowledge, the material and spiritual, the science and humanities, prehistory and history, antiquity and modernity, and so on. To take Pierre Bourdieu's call seriously, it encourages a move from *opus operatum* (result of practices) to *modus operandi* (mode of practices). Recalling the paradox mentioned in the introduction – that archaeology is dedicated to the lives of people but only has objects to study – in order to access the people of antiquity, we have to explore them via things. Because things once were, and still are, entangled to people, it is feasible to approach not just people's actions but, more broadly, their lives, thoughts, fears, and hopes in this way. As discussed in Section 3, interaction with things is what makes people, while in turn the process of reflecting on these kinds of entanglements shapes individual identities, as demonstrated in Section 4. Section 5 explored techniques of people's appropriation of the wider environment and finally, as shown in Section 6, cultural techniques create communities of people, even to the extent that entanglements with things makes past entities – even people – part of the present. Since technique is the practice of entanglement and technology is the science of entanglement, to paraphrase a famous archaeological saying:[38] archaeology is technology, or it is nothing.

---

[38] 'American archaeology is anthropology or it is nothing' (Willey & Phillips, 1958: 2) is a central creed of new archaeology.

References

Abd El Gawad, H. (2022). (Re)claiming the Rosetta: The Rosetta Stone and the (Re)writing of Egypt's Modern History. In *100 Histories of 100 Worlds in 1 Object*. https://100histories100worlds.org/reclaiming-the-rosetta/ (accessed 12 August 2022).

Allen, J. P. (2013). *The Ancient Egyptian Language*. Cambridge: Cambridge University Press.

Allen, J. P. (2014). *Middle Egyptian. Third Edition, Revised and Reorganized, with a New Analysis of the Verbal System*. Cambridge: Cambridge University Press.

Anderson, J. R. & Ahmed, S. M., eds. (2006). Bread Moulds and 'Throne Halls'. *SN* 10, 95–101.

Appadurai, A. (1996). *Modernity at Large*. Minneapolis: University of Minnesota Press.

Arnold, D. & Bourriau, J., eds. (1993). *An Introduction to Ancient Egyptian Pottery*. Mainz: Zabern.

Arpagaus, D. (2021). Mikrokosmos – Makrokosmos. In Quack, J. F. & Luft, D. C., eds., *Schrift und Material*. Tübingen: Mohr Siebeck, pp. 69–111.

Assmann, J. (1990). *Ma'at. Gerechtigkeit und Unsterblichkeit im alten Ägypten*. Munich: Beck.

Assmann, J. (1992). *Das kulturelle Gedächtnis*. Munich: Beck.

Assmann, J. (2009). *The Mosaic Distinction or The Price of Monotheism*. Palo Alto: Stanford University Press.

Assmann, J. (2018). *Achsenzeit. Eine Archäologie der Moderne*. Munich: Beck.

Assmann. A. & Assmann, J., eds. (2003). *Hieroglyphen. Stationen einer anderen abendländischen Grammatologie*, Archäologie der literarischen Kommunikation VIII, Munich: Fink.

Auenmüller, J., Verly, G., & Rademakers, F. W. (2019). Bronze Casting Artefacts from the Qubbet el-Hawa. In Verly, G., Rademakers, F. W., & Téreygeol F., eds., *Studies in Experimental Archaeometallurgy*. Drémil Lafage: Mergoil, pp. 141–57.

Aufrère, S. H. (2007). *Thot Hermes l'Egyptien*. Paris: L'Harmattan.

Austin, J. L. (1962). *How to Do Things with Words*. Oxford: Clarendon Press.

Bader, B. (2021a). *Material Culture and Identities in Egyptology*. Vienna: Austrian Academy of Science Press.

Bader, B. (2021b). Regional Differences in Pottery Repertoires: Two Case Studies of Early and Late Middle Kingdom Assemblages. In Jiménez-Serrano,

A. & Morales, A. J., eds., *Middle Kingdom Palace Culture and Its Echoes in the Provinces. Regional Perspectives and Realities*. HES 12. Leiden: Brill, pp. 45–76.

Bader, B. & Ownby, M. F., eds. (2013). *Functional Aspects of Egyptian Ceramics in their Archaeological Context*. OLA 217. Leuven: Peeters.

Bhabha, H. K. (2004). *The Location of Culture*. Abingdon: Routledge.

Baines, J. (1985). *Fecundity Figures*. Warminster: Aris & Phillips.

Baines, J. (2007). *Visual and Written Culture in Ancient Egypt*. Oxford: Oxford University Press.

Baligh, R. (2010). Complementary Medicine in Ancient and Modern Egypt. In Cockitt, J. & David, R., eds., *Pharmacy and Medicine in Ancient Egypt*. BAR IS 2141. Oxford: Archaeopress, pp. 6–10.

Balz, H. (2014). *Ngoe – Osiris – Aeneas*. Berlin: Lit.

Barbotin, C. (2005). *La voix des hiéroglyphes*. Paris: Khéops.

Barta, W. (1970). *Das Selbstzeugnis eines altägyptischen Künstlers*. MÄS 22. Berlin: Hessling.

Bats, A. (2020). The Production of Bread in Conical Moulds at the Beginning of the Egyptian Middle Kingdom. *JAS Reports*, 35. https://doi.org/10.1016/j .jasrep.2020.102631.

Baud, M. (1938). Le métier d'Irtisen, *CdE*, 13, 20–34.

Bauer, Th. (2011). *Die Kultur der Ambiguität*. Berlin: Verlage der Weltreligionen.

Bauer, Th. (2018). *Warum es kein islamisches Mittelalter gab*. Munich: Beck.

Beck, H. (2020). *Localism and the Ancient Greek City-State*. Chicago: University of Chicago Press.

Becker, J., Jungfleisch, J., & von Rüden, C., eds. (2018). *Tracing Technoscapes*. Leiden: Sidestone.

Bianchi, R. S. & Ziegler, Ch. (2014). *Egyptian Bronzes*. Bern: Schaap.

Blumenberg, H. (2009). *Geistesgeschichte der Technik*. Frankfurt: Suhrkamp.

Bonneau, D. (1964). *La Crue du Nil*. Paris: Klincksieck.

Bourdieu, P. (1977). *Outline of a Theory of Practice*. Cambridge: Cambridge University Press.

Bourriau, J. (2007). The Vienna System in Retrospect: How Useful Is It? In Hawass, Z. A. & Richards, J., eds., *The Archaeology and Art of Ancient Egypt. Essays in Honor of David B. O'Connor*. Cairo: SCA, pp. 137–44.

Bourriau, J. & Phillips, J., eds. (2004). *Invention and Innovation: The Social Context of Technological Change 2*. Oxford: Oxbow Books.

Bourriau, J., Nicholson, P., & Rose, P. (2000). Pottery. In Nicholson, P. & Shaw, I., eds., *Ancient Egyptian Materials and Technology*. Cambridge: Cambridge University Press, pp. 121–47.

Bowman, A. K., Crowther, Ch. V., Hornblower, S., Mairs, R., & Savvopoulos, K., eds. (2021). *Corpus of Ptolemaic Inscriptions*. Oxford: Oxford University Press.

Briant, P. (1999). Inscriptions multilingues d'époque achéménide. In Valbelle, D. & Leclant, J., eds., *Le décret de Memphis*. Paris: De Boccard, pp. 91–115.

Brugsch, H. (1880). *Hieroglyphisch-Demotisches Wörterbuch V*. Leipzig: Hinrichs.

Bryan, B. M. (2017). Art-Making in Texts and Contexts. In Jasnow, R. & Widmer, Gh., eds., *Illuminating Osiris. Egyptological Studies in Honor of Mark Smith*. MVCAE 2. Atlanta: Lockwood, pp. 1–21.

Buchwald, J. & Greco Josefowicz, D. (2020). *The Riddle of the Rosetta*. Princeton: Princeton University Press.

de Buck, A. (1961). *The Egyptian Coffin Texts VII*. OIP 87. Chicago: The Oriental Institute.

Budge, E. A. W. (1911). *The Egyptian Religion of the Resurrection*. London: Warner.

Budka, J. (2020). *AcrossBorders 2. Living in New Kingdom Sai*. AESL 1. Vienna: Austrian Academy of Sciences.

Burmeister, St. & Bernbeck, R., eds. (2017). *The Interplay of People and Technologies. Archaeological Case Studies on Innovations*. Berlin Studies of the Ancient World 43. Berlin: Topoi.

Burmeister, St., Hansen, S., Kunst, M., & Müller-Scheeßel, N., eds. (2013). *Metal Matters*. Rahden: VML.

Burstein, S. M. (1989). *Agatharchides of Cnidos. On the Erythrean Sea*. London: Taylor & Francis.

Butzer, K. W. (1976). *Early Hydraulic Civilization in Egypt*. Chicago: University of Chicago Press.

Cancik-Kirschbaum, E. & Traninger, A., eds. (2015). *Wissen in Bewegung. Institution – Iteration – Transfer. Episteme in Bewegung*. Wiesbaden: Harrassowitz.

Carlig, N., Lescuyer, G., Motte, A., & Sijic, N., eds. (2020). *Signes dans les textes*. Liège: Presses Universitaires de Liège.

Cauville, S. (1997a). *Le temple de Dendara. Les chapelles osiriennes*. Dendara X. Cairo: IFAO.

Cauville, S. (1997b). *Le Temple de Dendara. Les chapelles osiriennes. Transcription et traduction*. BdÉ 117. Cairo: IFAO.

Cauville, S. (1997c). *Le Temple de Dendara. Les chapelles osiriennes. Commentaire*. BdÉ 118. Cairo: IFAO.

Centrone, M. (2009). *Egyptian Corn-Mummies*. Saarbrücken: Müller.

Chassinat, É. (1966/8). *Le mystère d'Osiris au mois de Khoiak*. Cairo: IFAO.

Cockitt, J. & David, R., eds. (2010). *Pharmacy and Medicine in Ancient Egypt*. BAR IS 2141. Oxford: Archaeopress.

Colla, E. (2007). *Conflicted Antiquities*. Durham: Duke University Press.

Crellin, R. (2020). *Change and Archaeology*. Themes in Archaeology. Abingdon: Routledge/Taylor & Francis Group.

Crystal, D. (2010). *Die Cambridge Enzyklopädie der Sprache*. Berlin: Haffmanns & Tolkemitt.

Darnell, J. C. (2004). *The Enigmatic Netherworld Books of the Solar-Osirian Unity*. OBO 198. Fribourg: Academic Press/Göttingen: Vandenhoek & Ruprecht.

Daumas, F. (1983). L'Alchimi a-t-elle une origine égyptienne? In Grimm, G., Heinen, H., & Winter, E., eds., *Das Römisch-Byzantinische Ägypten*. Mainz: Zabern, pp. 109–18.

David, R. A., ed. (1986). *Science in Egyptology*, Manchester: Manchester University Press.

Davies, V. & Laboury, D., eds. (2020). *The Oxford Handbook of Egyptian Epigraphy and Palaeography*. Oxford: Oxford University Press.

Davies, W. V. & Walker, R., eds. (1993). *Biological Anthropology and the Study of Ancient Egypt*. London: British Museum Press.

Dawson, J., Rozeik, C., & Wright, M. M., eds. (2010). *Decorated Surfaces on Ancient Egyptian Objects*. London: Archetype Publications.

Dawson, W. R. (1953). Egypt's Place in Medical History. In Underwood, E. A., ed., *Science, Medicine and History*. London: Oxford University Press, pp. 47–60.

Depraetere, D. D. E. (2002). A Comparative Study on the Construction and the Use of the Domestic Bread Oven in Egypt during the Graeco-Roman and Late Antique/Early Byzantine Period, *MDAIK* 58, 119–56.

Derrida, J. (1997). *Of Grammatology*. Baltimore: Johns Hopkins University Press.

Douglas, M. (1966). *Purity and Danger*. New York: Routledge.

Downs, J. (2020). *Discovery at Rosetta*. 2nd ed. Cairo: AUC Press.

Doyon, W. (2015). On Archaeological Labor in Modern Egypt. In Carruthers, W., ed., *Histories of Egyptology*. New York: Routledge, pp. 141–56.

Drioton, É. & Fairman, H. W., eds. (1992). *Cryptographie ou pages sur le développement de l'alphabet en Égypte ancienne*. CASAE 28. Cairo: SCA.

Durkheim, E. (1915). *The Elementary Forms of the Religious Life*. London: Allen & Unwin.

Ebeling, F. (2014). Ägypten als Heimat der Alchemie. In Feuerstein-Herz, P. & Laube, S., eds. *Die Alchemie*. Wiesbaden: Harrassowitz, pp. 23–34.

Eckmann, C. & Shafik, S. (2002). *Die beiden Kupferstatuen des Pepi I. aus dem Tempel von Hierakonpolis in Ägypten.* Mainz: RGZ.

El Hawary, A. (2015). Stille Gedichte. In Morenz, L. D. & El Hawary, A., eds., *Weitergabe. Festschrift für Ursula Rössler-Köhler zum 65. Geburtstag.* GOF 53. Wiesbaden: Harrassowitz, pp. 153–66.

El-Hawary, A. (2018). Epistemological Things! Mystical Things! Towards an Ancient Egyptian Ontology. In Miniaci, G., Moreno García, J. C., Quirke, S. & Stauder, A., eds., *The Arts of Making in Ancient Egypt.* Leiden: Sidestone Press, pp. 67–9.

Eliade, M. (1978). *The Forge and The Crucible.* Chicago: University of Chicago Press.

Endesfelder, E. (1979). Zur Frage der Bewässerung im pharaonischen Ägypten. *ZÄS* 106, pp. 37–51.

Épron, L. & Daumas, F. (1939). *Le Tombeau de Ti I.* MIFAO 65. Cairo: IFAO.

Faltings, D. (1991). Die Bierbrauerei im AR. *ZÄS* 118, pp. 104–16.

Faltings, D. (1995). bS# und zwt – zwei ungeklärte Begriffe der Getreidewirtschaft im AR. *GM* 148, pp. 35–44.

Faltings, D. (1998). *Die Keramik der Lebensmittelproduktion im Alten Reich.* SAGA 14, Heidelberg: Orientverlag.

Feisal, A. E., ed. (1995). *Proceedings of the First International Conference on Ancient Egyptian Mining, Metallurgy and Conservation of Metallic Artefacts.* Cairo: SCA.

Feuerbach, L. (1975). Die Naturwissenschaft und die Revolution (1850). In: Feuerbach. L. *Werke* 4. Frankfurt a. M.: Suhrkamp, pp. 243–65.

Fischer-Elfert, H.-W. (2002). Das verschwiegene Wissen des Irtisen. In Assmann, J. & Bommas, M., eds., *Ägyptische Mysterien?* Munich: Fink, pp. 27–35.

Fischer-Elfert, H. (2005). *Abseits von Ma'at.* WSA 1. Würzburg: Ergon.

Fischer-Lichte, E. (2005). Performativität/performativ. In Fischer-Lichte, E., Kolesch, D. & Warstat, M., eds., *Metzler Lexikon Theatertheorie.* Stuttgart: Metzler, pp. 234–42.

Fitzenreiter, M. (2014). Metall und Kultur – Eine kurze Geschichte der 'thermischen Revolution'. In Fitzenreiter, M., Loeben, Ch. E., Raue, D. & Wallenstein, U., eds., *Gegossene Götter. Metallhandwerk und Massenproduktion im Alten Ägypten.* Rahden: Verlag Marie Leidorf, pp. 31–29.

Fitzenreiter, M. (2015). (Un)Zugänglichkeit. In Kehnel, A. & Panagiotopoulos, D., eds., *Schriftträger – Textträger.* Berlin: de Gruyter, pp. 179–208.

Fitzenreiter, M. (2019). Schon wieder Stele Louvre C 14 des Irtisen. *GM* 257, pp. 49–61.

Fitzenreiter, M. (2020). *Technologie und / als / eine Kulturwissenschaft*. Berlin: EB-Verlag.

Fitzenreiter, M. (2021). Ehrenwerte Töpfe und ihre Potenzen. Zu Qrḥ.t Sps in den Choiak-Inschriften und anderswo. *SAK* 50. pp. 109–131.

Fitzenreiter, M. (in press). Geheimnis ist Veränderung. Zu St# und s.St#, in press.

Fitzenreiter, M., Loeben, Ch. E., Raue, D. & Wallenstein, U., eds. (2014). *Gegossene Götter*. Rahden: VML.

Fitzenreiter, M., Willer, F. & Auenmüller, J. (2016). *Materialien einer Gusswerkstatt von der Qubbet el-Hawa*. Berlin: EB-Verlag.

Fleck, L. (1935). *Entstehung und Entwicklung einer wissenschaftlichen Tatsache*. Basel: Schwabe und Co.

Florès, J. (2015). *Les céréales*. BSAK 17. Hamburg: Buske.

Foucault, M. (1963). *Naissance de la clinique*. Paris: Presses universitaires de France.

Fox, R., Panagiotopoulos, D. & Tsouparopoulou, Ch. (2015). Affordanz. In Ott, M. R., Sauer, R., & Meier, Th., eds., *Materiale Textkulturen*. Berlin / Boston / Munich: De Gruyter, pp. 63–70.

Frazer, J. G. (1914). *Adonis, Attis, Osiris*. London: Macmillian.

French, P. G. (2016). Why does Egyptian Pottery Change? In Bader, B., Knoblauch, C. M., & Köhler, E. C., eds., *Vienna 2 – Ancient Egyptian Ceramics in the 21st Century*. OLA 245. Leuven: Peeters, pp. 203–9.

Frese,T., Hornbacher, A., & Willer, L. (2015). Präsenz. In Meier, Th., Ott, M. R., & Sauer, R., eds., *Materiale Textkulturen. Konzepte – Materialien – Praktiken*. Materiale Textkulturen 1. Berlin/Boston/ München: de Gruyter, pp. 87–100.

Fuller, D. Q. & Lucas, L. (2020). Savanna on the Nile. In Emberling, G. & Williams, B. B., eds., *The Oxford Handbook of Ancient Nubia*. Oxford: Oxford University Press, pp. 927–53.

Gaillhard, N. (2018). Experimental Archaeology on Metals. DOI: 10.19080/ GJAA.218.03.555622. (25.05.2021)

Ghalioungui, P. (1963). *Magic and Medical Science in Ancient Egypt*. New York: Barnes & Noble.

Goebs, K. (2007). King as God and God as King. In Gundlach, R., Kreikenbom, D. & Spence, K., eds., *Palace and Temple*. Wiesbaden: Harrassowitz, pp. 57–101.

Goebs, K. & Baines, J. (2018). Functions and Uses of Egyptian Myths. In Medini L. & Tallet, G., eds., *Qu'est-ce qu'un mythe égyptien? / What is an Egyptian Myth?* Paris: Colin, pp. 645–77.

Geoghegan, B. D. (2013). After Kittler: On the Cultural Techniques of Recent German Media Theory. Theory, *Culture & Society* 30(6), pp. 66–72.

Goldsmith, D. (2022). Smellscapes in Ancient Egypt. In Neumann, K. & Thomason, A., eds., *The Routledge Handbook of the Senses of the Ancient Near East*. Abingdon: Routledge, pp. 636–62.

Graf, J. & Krutzsch, M., eds. (2008). *Ägypten lesbar machen – die klassische Konservierung/Restaurierung von Papyri und neuere Verfahren*. AfP Beiheft 24. Berlin: Walter de Gruyter.

Graff, G. & Jimenez Serrano, A., eds. (2015). *Préhistoires de l'écriture*. Marsailles: Presses Universitaires de Provence.

Grapow, H. (1955). *Von den medizinischen Texten*. Berlin: Akademie-Verlag.

Grapow, H., von Deines, H. & Westendorf, W. (1954–1973). *Grundriss der Medizin der alten Ägypter* I-IX. Berlin: Akademie-Verlag.

Graves-Brown, C. & Goodridge, W., eds. (2015). *Egyptology in the Present*. Swansea: The classical Press of Wales.

Griffiths, J. G. (1970). *Plutarch's De Iside Et Osiride*. Swansea: University of Wales Press.

Grube, G., Kogge, W. & Krämer, S. eds. (2005). *Schrift. Kulturtechnik zwischen Auge, Hand und Maschine*. München: Fink.

Guglielmi, W. (1991). *Die Göttin MR.T.* PdÄ 7. Leiden / New York / Kopenhagen / Köln: Brill.

Guglielmi, W. (1994). Die Biergöttin Menket. In Minas, M. & Zeidler, J., eds., *Aspekte spätägyptischer Kultur. Festschrift für Erich Winter zum 65. Geburtstag*. AegTrev 7. Mainz: Zabern.

Hahn, H.-P. (2015). *Vom Eigensinn der Dinge*. Berlin: Nefolis.

Hahn, H.-P. (2019). The Values of Things, Pragmatically, Symbolically and Emotionally: Some Remarks on Object Appreciation. In Jaritz, G. & Matschinegg, I., eds., *My Favourite Things: Object Preferences in Medieval and Early Modern Material Culture*. Berlin: LIT, pp. 21–35.

Haraway, D. (1991). A Cyborg Manifesto. In Haraway, D. *Simians, Cyborgs and Women*. New York; Routledge, pp. 149–81.

Haring, B. (2018). *From Single Sign to Pseudo-Script*. CANE 93. Leiden / Boston: Brill.

Harman, G. (2018). *Object-Orientated Ontology: A New Theory of Everything*. Westminster: Penguin.

Harris, R. (1995). *Signs of Writing*. London & New York: Routledge.

Hayden, B., Nixon-Darcus, L., & Ansell, L. (2017). Our 'Daily Bread'? In Steel, L., & Zinn, K., eds., *Exploring the Materiality of Food 'Stuffs'*. London / New York: Routledge, pp. 57–78.

Haywood, P. (2017). The Ontological Turn. In Stein, F. et al., eds., *The Cambridge Encyclopedia of Anthropology*. doi.org/10.29164/17ontology

Hegel, G. W. F. (1975). *Wissenschaft der Logik I*. Hamburg: Meiner.

Helck, W. (1971). *Das Bier im Alten Ägypten*. Berlin: Institut für Gärungsgewerbe und Biotechnologie.

Hendrickx, S., Faltings, D., Op de Beeck, L., Raue, D. & Michiels, Ch. (2002). Milk, Beer and Bread Technology During the Early Dynastic Period, *MDAIK* 58, pp. 277–304.

Hessler, M. (2012). *Kulturgeschichte der Technik*. Frankfurt: Campus.

Hobsbawm, E. & Ranger, T., eds. (1983). *The Invention of Tradition*. Cambridge: Cambridge University Press.

Hodder, I. (2012). *Entangled. An Archaeology of the Relationships between Humans and Things*. Chichester: Wiley-Blackwell.

Hodgkinson, A. K. & Tvetmarken, C. L., eds. (2020), *Approaches to the Analysis of Production Activity at Archaeological Sites*. Oxford: Archaeopress.

Hoffmann, F., Minas-Nerpel, M., & Pfeiffer, St. (2009). *Die dreisprachige Stele des C. Cornelius Gallus*. AfP Beiheft 9, Berlin: De Gruyter.

Hoffmann, F. & Pfeiffer, St. (2021). *Der Stein von Rosetta: Neuübersetzung des Rosetta-Textes*. Stuttgart: Reclam.

Holthoer, R. (1977). *New Kingdom Pharaonic Sites. The Pottery*. SJE 5:1, Copenhagen: Scandinavian University Books.

Honneth, A. (2015). *Verdinglichung. Eine erkennungstheoretische Studie*. Berlin: Suhrkamp.

Hornung, E. (1999). *Das esoterische Ägypten*. Munich: Beck.

Horton, R. (1993). *Patterns of Thought in Africa and the West*. Cambridge: Cambridge University Press.

Humbert, J. (1989). *L'égyptomanie dans l'art occidental*. Paris: ACR Édition.

Ikram, S., Kaiser, J., & Walker, R., eds. (2015). *Egyptian Bioarchaeology*. Leiden: Sidestone Press.

Jacquet-Gordon, H. (1981). A Tentative Typology of Egyptian Bread Moulds. In D. Arnold ed. *Studien zur altägyptischen Keramik*. DAI Sonderschrift 9. Mainz: Zabern, pp. 11–24.

Kaczmarczyk, A. (1983). *Ancient Egyptian Faience*. Warminster: Aris & Phillips Ltd.

Kahl, J. (1994). *Das System der ägyptischen Hieroglyphenschrift in der 0.-3. Dynastie*. GOF 29. Wiesbaden: Harrassowitz.

Kalthoff, H., Cress T., & Röhl, T., eds. (2016). *Materialität*. Paderborn: Fink.

Kamal, A. Bey (1904). *Stèles ptolemaiques et romaines. CG 22001–22208,*. Cairo: Imprimerie IFAO.

Kammerzell, F. (2021). Reading Multimodal Compositions from Early Dynastic Egypt (with an Appendix on Previously Unlisted, Reinterpreted or Otherwise Noteworthy Signs). In Engel, E.-M., Blöbaum, A. I., &

Kammerzell, F., eds., *Keep out! Early Dynastic and Old Kingdom Cylinder Seals and Sealings in Context*. Menes 7. Wiesbaden: Harrassowitz, pp. 1–98.

Karenberg, A. & Leitz, Ch., eds. (2002). *Heilkunde und Hochkultur II*. Münster: LIT.

Kassung, Ch. (2009). *Die Unordnung der Dinge*. Bielefeld: Transcript.

Kassung, Ch. & Macho, Th. eds. (2013). *Kulturtechniken der Synchronisation*. München: Fink.

Kehnel, A. & Panagiotopoulos, D., eds. (2015). *Schriftträger – Textträger*. Berlin: de Gruyter.

Kemp, B. & Stevens, A. (2010). *Busy Lives at Amarna*. London: EES.

Killen, G. (2017). *Ancient Egyptian Furniture*. Oxford: Oxbow Books.

Kittler, F. (1985). *Aufschreibesysteme 1800/1900*. München: Fink.

Klotz, D. & Stauder, A., eds. (2020). *Enigmatic Writing in the New Kingdom*. ZÄS Beihefte 12.1. Berlin: de Gruyter.

Knopes, J. (2019). Science, Technology, and Human Health: The Value of STS in Medical and Health Humanities Pedagogy. In *Journal of Medical Humanities* 40(2), DOI:10.1007/s10912-019-09551-3. (25.05.2021).

Kuhn, Th. S. (1970). *The Structure of Scientific Revolutions*. 2nd ed. Chicago: University of Chicago Press.

Kuijpers, M. H. G. (2018). *An Archaeology of Skill*. New York: Routledge.

Lane, E. W. (1890). *An Account of the Manners and Customs of the Modern Egyptians. (Written in Egypt During the Years 1833–1835)*. London: Ward, Lock and Co.

Latour, B. (1993). *We have never been modern*. Cambridge, Mass.: Harvard University Press.

Latour, B. (2000). On the Partial Existence of Existing and Nonexisting Objects. In Daston, L., ed., *Biographies of Scientific Objects*. Chicago: Chicago University Press, pp. 247–69.

Latour, B. (2005). *Reassembling the Social*. Oxford: Oxford University Press.

Lehner, M. (1996). Pyramid Age Bakery Reconstructed. *AERAgram* 1(1), pp. 6–7.

Leitz, Ch. (2017). Das Menu-Lied. In Jasnow, R. & Widmer, G., eds., *Illuminating Osiris. Egyptological Studies in Honor of Mark Smith*. MVCAE 2. Atlanta: Lockwood, pp. 221–37.

Lepsius, R. (1849–59). *Denkmaeler aus Aegypten und Aethiopien*. Berlin: Nicolai.

Leroi-Gourhan, A. (1992). *Évolution et techniques*. Paris: Michel.

Lévi-Strauss, C. (1962). *La pensée sauvage*. Paris: plon.

von Lieven, A. (2004). Das Göttliche in der Natur erkennen. Tiere, Pflanzen und Phänomene der unbelebten Natur als Manifestationen des Göttlichen. *ZÄS* 131, pp. 156–72.

Lucarelli, R. (2010). The Guardian-Demons of the Book of the Dead. *BMSAES* 15, pp. 85–102.

Lucas, A. (1926). *Ancient Egyptian Materials and Industries*. London: Arnold, Longmans, Green & Co.

Lucas, A. (1962). *Ancient Egyptian Materials and* Industries. Fourth edition, revised and enlarged by J.R. Harris. London: Edward Arnold.

Luhmann, N. (1987). *Soziale Systeme: Grundriss einer allgemeinen Theorie*. Frankfurt a. M.: Suhrkamp.

Maggetti, M. (2006). Archaeometry: Quo vadis? *Geological Society London Special Publications* 257(1), pp. 1–8.

Maier, M. (1617 / 1687). *Atalanta fugiens*. Oppenheim: de Bry.

Maran, J. & Stockhammer, P., eds. (2017). *Appropriating Innovations: Entangled Knowledge in Eurasia, 5000–1500 BCE*. Oxford Haverton, PA: Oxbow Books.

Marcus Aurelius Antoninus (1992). *Meditations*. New York: Knopf.

Mariette, A. (1871). *Dendérah IV. Terrasses*. Paris: n.p.

Marx, K. (1962). *Das Kapital I*. MEW 23. Berlin: Dietz.

Mathieu, B., Meeks, D., & Wissa, M., eds. (2006). *L'apport de l'Égypte à l'histoire des techniques*. BdE 142, Cairo: IFAO.

Matić, U. (2020). *Ethnic Identities in the Land of the Pharaos*. Ancient Egypt in Context. Cambridge: Cambridge University Press.

Mauelshagen, F. (2007). Warten auf Champollion? In Glück, Th. & Morenz, L. D., eds., *Exotisch, Weisheitlich und Uralt*. Hamburg: Lit, pp. 57–80.

McLuhan, M. (1962). *The Gutenberg Galaxy. The Making of Typographic Man*. Toronto: University of Toronto Press.

McLuhan, M. (1964). *Understanding Media: The Extensions of Man*. New York: Hill.

McLuhan, M. (1967). *The Medium is the Massage: An Inventory of Effects*. London: Penguin.

Meeks, D. (2006). L'Égypte ancienne et l'histoire des techniques. In Mathieu, B., Meeks, D., & Wissa, M., eds., *L'apport de l'Égypte à l'histoire des techniques*. BdE 142, Kairo: IFAO, pp. 1–13.

Meskell, L. (2004). *Object Worlds in Ancient Egypt*. Oxford: Berg.

Michels, S. (2013). Kornosiris – Osirisbeet. In Neunert, G., Gabler, K., & Verbovsek, A., eds., *Nekropolen: Grab – Bild – Ritual*. GOF 54. Wiesbaden: Harrassowitz, pp. 161–79.

Minas-Nerpel, M. (2019). 'Seeing Double'. Intercultural Dimensions of the Royal Ideology in Ptolemaic Egypt. In Budka, J., ed., *Egyptian royal ideology and kingship under periods of foreign rulers*. KSGH 4,6. Wiesbaden: Harrassowitz, pp. 189–205.

Miniaci, G. (2021). The Craft of Non-Mechanically Reproducible: Targeting Centres of Faience Figurin Production in 1800–1650 BC Egypt. In Jiménez-Serrano, A. & Morales, A.J., eds., *Middle Kingdom Palace Culture and Its Echoes in the Provinces. Regional Perspectives and Realities*. HES 12, Leiden: Brill, pp. 284–329.

Miniaci, G., Moreno García, J. C., Quirke, S. & Stauder, A. (2018). *The Arts of Making in Ancient Egypt*. Leiden: Sidestone Press.

Moreno García, J. C. (2015). The Cursed Discipline? In W. Carruthers, ed., *Histories of Egyptology*. RSE 2. New York: Routledge, pp. 50–63.

Moreno García, J. C., ed. (2016). *Dynamics of Production in the Ancient Near East 1300–500BC*. Oxford: Oxbow.

Morenz, L. (2004). *Bild-Buchstaben und symbolische Zeichen*. OBO 205. Fribourg & Göttingen: Academic Press/Vandenhoeck & Ruprecht.

Morenz, L. (2008). *Sinn und Spiel der Zeichen*. Köln: Böhlau.

Morenz, L. & Schorsch, S., eds. (2007). *Was ist ein Text?* Berlin: De Gruyter.

Morenz, L. D. (1996). *Beiträge zur Schriftlichkeitskultur im Mittleren Reich und der 2. Zwischenzeit*. ÄAT 29. Wiesbaden: Harrassowitz.

Morenz, L. D. (2020) *Von Kennen und Können*. THOT 5. Berlin: EB-Verlag.

Morenz, L. D. (2021). *VerLautung von Macht*. Berlin: EB-Verlag.

Morris, W. et al. (1893). *Arts and Crafts Essays*. London: Rivington, Percival, & Co.

Mourad, A.-L. (2021). *The Enigma of the Hyksos Volume II. Transforming Egypt into the New Kingdom. The Impact of the Hyksos and Egyptian-Near Eastern Relations*, CAENL 10. Wiesbaden: Harrassowitz.

Müller-Wollermann, R. (2021). *Einführung in die altägyptische Wirtschaft*. Einführungen und Quellentexte zur Ägyptologie 13. Berlin: Lit.

Nicholson, P. T. (2010). 'Other Than' – Egyptology as Science? In Cockitt, J. & David, R., eds., *Pharmacy and Medicine in Ancient Egypt*. BAR IS 2141. Oxford: Archaeopress, pp. 122–26.

Nicholson, P. T. & Doherty, S. K. (2016). Arts and Crafts: Artistic Representations as Ethno-Archaeology. In Bader, B., Knoblauch, C. M., & Köhler, E. C., eds., *Vienna 2 – Ancient Egyptian Ceramics in the 21st Century*. OLA 245. Leuven: Peeters, pp. 703–22.

Nunn, J. F. (1996). *Ancient Egyptian Medicine*. London: British Museum Press.

Nyord, R. (2020). *Seeing Perfection. Ancient Egyptian Images beyond Representation*. Ancient Egypt in Context. Cambridge: Cambridge University Press.

O'Brien, M. J. & Lyman, R. L. (2000). *Applying Evolutionary Archaeology: A Systematic Approach*. New York: Kluwer Academic/Plenum.

Odler, M. & Kmošek, J. (2020). *Invisible Connections.* AE 31. Oxford, Archaeopress.

Parker Pearson, M. (2003). Food, Identity and Culture. In Parker Pearson, M., ed. *Food, Culture and Identity in the Neolithic and Early Bronze Age.* BAR IS 1117. Oxford: Archaeopress, pp. 1–30.

Parkinson, R. (2002). *Poetry and Culture in Middle Kingdom Egypt.* New York: Continuum.

Parkinson, R. (2005). *The Rosetta Stone.* London: BM Press.

Petrie, W. M. F. (1892). *Ten Years' Digging in Egypt 1881 – 1891.* London: The Religious Tract Society.

Petrie, W. M. F. (1901). *Diospolis Parva. The Cemeteries of Abadiyeh and Hu 1898–9.* London.

Petrie, W. M. F. (1910). *The Arts & Crafts of Ancient Egypt.* London & Edinburgh: Foulis.

Petrie, W. M. F. (1914). *Amulets.* London: Constable.

Petrie, W. M. F. (1917a). *Tools and Weapons.* London: Constable.

Petrie, W. M. F. (1917b). *Scarabs and Cylinders with Names.* London: Constable.

Petrie, W. M. F. (1927). *Objects of Daily Use.* London: Constable.

Pfeifer, W. (2011). *Etymologisches Wörterbuch des Deutschen.* Koblenz: Edition Kramer.

Pfeiffer, K. (2012). *Neue Untersuchungen zur Archäometallurgie des Sinai.* Menschen – Kulturen – Traditionen 11, Rahden: VML

Pfeiffer, S. (2004). *Das Dekret von Kanopos (238 v. Chr).* AfP Beiheft 18. Munich / Leipzig: Saur.

Pinarello, M. S. (2015). *An Archaeological Discussion of Writing Practice. Deconstruction of the Ancient Egyptian Scribe.* GHP Egyptology 23. London: GHP.

Piquette, K. E. (2018). *An Archaeology of Art and Writing. Early Egyptian Lables in Context.* Cologne: Modern Academic Publishing.

Polanyi, M. (1966). *The Tacit Dimension.* London: Routledge.

Pomian, K. (1984). *L'Ordre du temps.* Paris: Éditions Gallimard.

Pommerening, T. (2017). *Medical Re-enactments.* In Rosati, G. & Guidotti, M. C., eds., *Proceedings of the XI International Congress of Egyptologists.* AE 15. Oxford: Archaeopress, pp. 519–26.

Prell, S. (2011). *Einblicke in die Werkstätten der Residenz. Die Stein- und Metallwerkzeuge des Grabungsplatzes Q 1.* FR 8. Hildesheim: Gerstenberg.

Prentiss, A. M. ed. (2019). *Handbook of Evolutionary Research in Archaeology.* Heidelberg: Springer Nature.

Pusch, E. B. & Rehren, Th. (2007). *Hochtemperatur-Technologie in der Ramses-Stadt. Rubinglas für den Pharao.* FR 6. Hildesheim: Gerstenberg.

Quack, J. F. (2007). Saatprobe und Kornosiris. In Fitzenreiter, M., ed., *Das Heilige und die Ware*. IBAES VII. London: GHP, pp. 325–31.

Quack, J. F. & Luft, D. C., eds. (2021). *Schrift und Material*. ORA 41. Tübingen: Mohr Siebeck.

Quirke, S. (2004). *Egyptian Literature 1800 BC: Questions and Readings*. London: Golden House Publications.

Quirke, S. (2010). *Hidden Hands: Egyptian Workforces in Petrie Excavation Archives, 1880–1924*. London: Duckworth.

Quirke, S. (2018). Languages of Artists: Closed and Open Channels. In Miniaci, G., Moreno García, J. C., Quirke, S., & Stauder, A., eds., *The Arts of Making in Ancient Egypt*. Leiden: Sidestone Press, pp. 175–96.

Quirke, S. & Andrews, C. (1988). *The Rosetta Stone*. London: British Museum.

Rademakers, F. W., Verly, G., Téreygeold, F., & Auenmüller, J. (2021). Contributions of Experimental Archaeology to Excavation and Material Studies. *JAS Reports* 38. https://doi.org/10.1016/j.jasrep.2021.103036

Radestock, S. (2015). *Prinzipien der ägyptischen Medizin*. WSA 4. Würzburg: Ergon Verlag.

Ragazzoli, C. (2019). *Scribes. Les artisans du texte en Égypte ancienne*. Paris: Les Belles Lettres.

Rashwan, H. (2019). Ancient Egyptian Image-Writing: Between the Unspoken and Visual Poetics, *JARCE* 55, pp. 137–160.

Raven, M. J. (1982). Corn-Mummies. *OMRO* 63, pp. 7–38.

Raven, M. J. (1983). Wax in Egyptian Magic and Symbolism. *OMRO* 64, pp. 7–47.

Raven, M. J. (1998). A New Type of Osiris Burials. In Clarysse, W., Schoors, A., & Willems, H., eds., *Egyptian Religion: The Last Thousand Years. Studies Dedicated to the Memory of Jan Quaegebeur*. OLA 84. Leuven: Peeters, pp. 227–39.

Ray, J. (2008). *The Rosetta Stone and the Rebirth of Ancient Egypt*. Harvard: Harvard University Press.

Regulski, I. (2020a). *Repurposing Ritual. Pap. Berlin P. 10480–82: A Case Study from Middle Kingdom Asyut*. ÄOPH 5. Berlin: De Gruyter.

Regulski, I. (2020b). The Rosetta Stone. Copying an Ancient Copy. In Davies, V. & Laboury, D., eds., *The Oxford Handbook of Egyptian Epigraphy and Palaeography*. Oxford: Oxford University Press, pp. 215–28.

Reid, D. M. (2015). *Contesting Antiquity in Egypt*. Cairo: AUC Press.

Rheinberger, H.-J. (1997). *Toward a History of Epistemic Things*. Stanford: Stanford University Press.

Richter, S. (2010). Naturoffenbarung und Erkenntnisritual. In Knuf, H., Leitz, C., & von Recklinghausen, D., eds., *Honi soit qui mal y pense*.

Studien zum pharaonischen, griechisch-römischen und spätantiken Ägypten zu Ehren von Heinz-Josef Thissen. OLA 149. Leuven: Peeters, pp. 585–605.

Roeder, G. (1933). Die Herstellung von Wachsmodellen zu ägyptischen Bronzefiguren. *ZÄS* 69, pp. 45–67.

Roeder, G. (1956). *Ägyptische Bronzefiguren.* Staatliche Museen zu Berlin. Berlin: Akademie Verlag.

Roeder, H. (2003), Die Imagination des Unsichtbaren. Die altägyptischen Erzählungen des Papyrus Westcar und die Performanz des Performativen. In Ulf, Ch. & Zirfas, J., eds., *Rituelle Welten.* Paragrana 12. Berlin: De Gruyter, pp. 184–222.

Roßler, G. (2008). Kleine Galerie neuer Dingbegriffe: Hybriden, Quasi-Objekte, Grenzobjekte, epistemische Dinge. In Kneer, G., Schroer, M., & Schüttpelz, E., eds., *Bruno Latours Kollektive.* Berlin: Suhrkamp, pp. 76–107.

Rowley-Conwy, P. (2007). *From Genesis to Prehistory: The Archaeological Three Age System and Its Contested Reception in Denmark, Britain, and Ireland.* Oxford: Oxford University Press.

Ryan, P. (2016). From Raw Resources to Food Processing. In Steel, L. & Zinn, K., eds., *Exploring the Materiality of Food 'Stuffs'.* RSA 23. London: Routledge, pp. 15–38.

Samuel, D. (1996). Archaeology of Ancient Egyptian Beer. *JASBC* 54(1), pp. 3–12.

Samuel, D. (1999). Brewing and Baking in Ancient Egyptian Art. In H. Walker, ed., *Food in the Arts.* Totnes, Devon: Prospect Books, pp. 173–81.

Samuel, D. (2000). Brewing and Baking. In Shaw, I. & Nicholson, P., eds., *Ancient Egyptian Materials and Technology.* Cambridge: Cambridge University Press, pp. 537–76.

Saussure, F. de (1959). *Course in General Linguistics.* New York: New York Philosophical Library.

Scheel, B. (1985). Studien zum Metallhandwerk im Alten Ägypten I. Handlungen und Beischriften in den Bildprogrammen der Gräber des Alten Reiches. *SAK* 12, pp. 117–77.

Scheel, B. (1986). Studien zum Metallhandwerk im Alten Ägypten II. Handlungen und Beischriften in den Bildprogrammen der Gräber des Mittleren Reiches. *SAK* 13, pp. 181–205.

Scheel, B. (1987). Studien zum Metallhandwerk im Alten Ägypten III. Handlungen und Beischriften in den Bildprogrammen der Gräber des Neuen Reiches und der Spätzeit. *SAK* 14, pp. 247–64.

Schenkel, W. (1965). *Memphis – Herakleopolis –Theben.* ÄA 12. Wiesbaden: Harrassowitz.

Schenkel, W. (1978). *Die Bewässerungsrevolution im Alten Ägypten*. Mainz: Zabern.

Schorsch, D. (1988). Technical Examinations of Ancient Egyptian Theriomorphic Hollow Cast Bronzes. In Watkins, S. C. & Brown, C. E., eds., *Conservation of Ancient Egyptian Materials*. London: British Museum Press, pp. 41–50.

von Schuler-Schörnig, I. (1972). *Werke indianischer Goldschmiedekunst*. Berlin: SMPK.

Schwechler, C. (2020). *Les noms des pains en Égypte ancienne*. SAK Beiheft 22. Hamburg: Buske.

Seidlmayer, St. J. (2000). *Zwischen Staatswirtschaft und Massenkonsum*. URN: urn: nbn:de:kobv:b4-opus-22131. http://edoc.bbaw.de/volltexte/2012/2213/ (accessed 24 May 2021).

Sennet, R. (2008). *The Craftsman*. New Haven, Conn.: Yale University Press.

Shaw, I. (2012). *Ancient Egyptian Technology and Innovation. Transformations in Pharaonic Material Culture*. Bristol: Bristol Classical Press.

Shaw, I. (2017). Technology in Transit. In Creasman, P. P. & Wilkinson, R. H., eds., *Pharao's Land and Beyond*. Oxford: Oxford University Press, pp. 167–80.

Shaw, I. & Nicholson, P. (2000). *Ancient Egyptian Materials and Technology*. Cambridge: Cambridge University Press.

Shortland, A. J. (2001). *The Social Context of Technological Change: Egypt and the Ancient Near East, 1650–1550 BC*. Oxford: Oxbow.

Siffert, U. (2021). Osiris – The Mummy *Par Excellence?* In Franci, M., Ikram, S., & Morfini, I., eds., *Rethinking Osiris*. SANEM 5. Rome: Arbor Sapentiae, pp. 175–88.

Sigl, J., Kopp, P., & Fritzsch, D. (2018). Stadt und Tempel von Elephantine – Methodological Approach to the Project 'Realities of Life' (Lebenswirklichkeiten). *MDAIK* 74, pp. 161–76.

Sjaastad, E. (2018). The Egyptian Reel. *SAK* 47, pp. 223–39.

Smith, M. (2017). *Following Osiris*. Oxford: Oxford University Press.

Smith, S. T. (2020).The Nubian Experience of Egyptian Domination During the New Kingdom. In Emberling, G. & Williams, B. B., eds., *The Oxford Handbook of Ancient Nubia*. Oxford: Oxford University Press, pp. 369–94.

Spinoza, B. (1677). *Ethica. Pars quarta – De servitute humana seu de affectuum viribus*. https://la.wikisource.org/wiki/Ethica/Pars_quarta_-_De_servitute_humana_seu_de_affectuum_viribus (accessed 24 May 2021).

Stauder, A. (2018). Staging Restricted Knowledge. In Miniaci, G., Moreno García, J. C., Quirke S., & Stauder, A., eds., *The Arts of Making in Ancient Egypt*. Leiden: Sidestone Press, pp. 238–71.

Steel, L. & Zinn, K., eds. (2017). *Exploring the Materiality of Food 'Stuffs'*. RSA 23. London: Routledge.

Stockhammer, Ph. W. (2013). From Hybridity to Entanglement, From Essentialism to Practice. In van Pelt W. P., ed., *Archaeology and Cultural Mixture*. ARC 28.1, pp. 11–28.

Stocks, D. A. (2003). *Experiments in Egyptian Archaeology. Stoneworking technology in Ancient Egpyt*. London: Routledge.

Strong, M. E. (2021). *Sacred Flames. The Power of Artificial Light in Ancient Egypt*. Cairo: AUC Press.

Strouhal, E., Vachala, B., & Vymazalová, H. (2014). *The Medicine of the Ancient Egyptians. 1: Surgery, Gynecology, Obstetrics, and Pediatrics*. Cairo: AUC Press.

Strouhal, E., Vachala, B., & Vymazalová, H. (2021). *The Medicine of the Ancient Egyptians. 2: Internal Medicine*. Cairo: AUC Press.

Thompson, D. J. (2018). Ptolemy I in Egypt: Continuity and Change. In McKechnie, P. & Cromwell, J. A., eds., *Ptolemy I and the Transformation of Egypt, 404–282 BCE*. Leiden: Brill, pp. 6–26.

Tiribilli, E. (2018). *The Bronze Figurines of the Petrie Museum from 2000 BC to AD 400*. GHP Egyptology 28. London: GHP.

Tooley, A. M. J. (1996). Osiris Bricks. *JEA* 82, pp. 167–79.

Trigger, B. G. (1989). *A History of Archaeological Thought*. Cambridge: Cambridge University Press.

Turner, B. S., ed. (2012). *Routledge Handbook of Body Studies*. London: Routledge.

Tylecote, R. F. (1992). *A History of Metallurgy*. Second Edition. London: Institute of Materials.

Valbelle, D. & Leclant, J., eds. (1999). *Le décret de Memphis*. Paris: De Boccard.

Van der Moezel, K. (2016). *Of Marks and Meaning: A Palaeographic, Semiotic-Cognitive, and Comparative Analysis of the Identity Marks from Deir el-Medina*. Leiden: PhD.

van Wolputte, S. & Fumanti, M., eds. (2010). *Beer in Africa*. African Studies 36. Münster: Lit.

Vandier, J. (1964). *Manuel d'Archéologie Egyptien IV*. Paris: Picard.

Veldmeijer, A. J. (2019). *The Ancient Egyptian Footwear Project*. Leiden: Sidestone Press.

Veldmeijer, A. J. & Ikram, S., eds. (2013). *Chasing Chariots*. Leiden: Sidestone Press.

Verhoeven, U. (1984). *Grillen, Kochen, Backen im Alltag und im Ritual Altägyptens*. Rites égyptiens IV. Brussels: Fondation Égyptologique Reine Élisabeth.

Vernus, P. (2017). Modelling the Relationship between Reproduction and Production of 'Sacralized' Texts in Pharaonic Egypt. In Todd, G., ed., *(Re)productive Traditions in Ancient Egypt*. AegLeo 10. Liège: Presses universitaires de Liège, pp. 149–61.

Versluys, M. J., ed. (2020). *Beyond Egyptomania*. Berlin: de Gruyter, 2020.

Vogelsang-Eastwood, G. (1993). *Pharaonic Egyptian Clothing*. Leiden: Brill.

Volokhine, Y. (2019). Les interdits alimentaires en Égypte ancienne. In Arnette, M.-L., ed., *Religion et alimentation en Égypte et Orient anciens*. RAPH 43. Cairo: IFAO, pp. 557–91.

Walker, J. (1990). The Place of Magic in the Practice of Medicine in Ancient Egypt. *BACE* 1, pp. 85–95.

Warden, L. A. (2014). *Pottery and Economy in Old Kingdom Egypt*. CHANE 65. Leiden: Brill.

Warden, L. A. (2021). *Ceramic Perspectives on Ancient Egyptian Society*. Ancient Egypt in Context. Cambridge: Cambridge University Press.

Weiss, K. (2012). *Ägyptische Tier- und Götterbronzen aus Unterägypten*. ÄAT 81. Wiesbaden: Harrassowitz.

Wendrich, W. (1999). *The World According to Basketry*. Leiden: Universiteit Leiden.

Wendrich, W. (2006). Body Knowledge. In Mathieu, B., Meeks, D., & Wissa, M. eds., *L'apport de l'Égypte à l'histoire des techniques*. BdE 142. Cairo: IFAO, pp. 267–75.

Westendorf, W. (1999). *Handbuch der altägyptischen Medizin*. HdO I.36. Leiden: Brill.

Wilde, H. (2003). *Technologische Innovationen im zweiten Jahrtausend vor Christus. Zur Verwendung und Verbreitung neuer Werkstoffe im ostmediterranen Raum*. GOF IV.44, Wiesbaden: Harrassowitz.

Wilde, H. (2011). *Innovation und Tradition*. GOF IV.49. Wiesbaden: Harrassowitz.

Wilkinson, J. G. (1837). *The Manners and Customs of the Ancient Egyptians, Including Their Private Life, Government, Laws, Arts, Manufactures, Religion, Agriculture, and Early History; Derived From a Comparison of the Paintings, Sculptures, and Monuments Still Existing, With the Accounts of Ancient Authors. Illustrated By Drawings of Those Subjects*. London: Murray.

Willems, H. (2003). Gärten in thebanischen Grabanlagen. In Meyer, S., ed., *Egypt – Temple of the Whole World. Ägypten – Tempel der gesamten Welt. Studies in Honour of Jan Assmann*. Leiden: Brill, pp. 421–39.

Willey, G. & Phillips, P. (1958). *Method and Theory in American Archaeology*. Chicago: Chicago University Press.

Willner, S., Koch, G. & Samida, S., ed. (2016). *Doing History.* Münster: Waxmann.

Winkler, H. (2015). *Prozessieren. Die dritte, vernachlässigte Medienfunktion.* Paderborn: Fink.

Zakrzewski, S., Shortland, A. & Rowland, J. (2016). *Science in the Study of Ancient Egypt.* RSE 3. London: Routledge.

Acknowledgements

My thanks go to the editors for their patience and indulgence with a text whose essence did not too neatly fit in the expected frame of content. Additional thanks go to the reviewers for their valuable comments. Special thanks are due to Anna Stevens and Ginevra House for taking on the English people's burden of proofreading and de-Germanising my English.

Cambridge Elements ☰

Ancient Egypt in Context

Gianluca Miniaci
University of Pisa

Gianluca Miniaci is Associate Professor in Egyptology at the University of Pisa, Honorary Researcher at the Institute of Archaeology, UCL – London, and Chercheur associé at the École Pratique des Hautes Études, Paris. He is currently co-director of the archaeological mission at Zawyet Sultan (Menya, Egypt). His main research interest focuses on the social history and the dynamics of material culture in the Middle Bronze Age Egypt and its interconnections between the Levant, Aegean, and Nubia.

Juan Carlos Moreno García
CNRS, Paris

Juan Carlos Moreno García (PhD in Egyptology, 1995) is a CNRS senior researcher at the University of Paris IV-Sorbonne, as well as lecturer on social and economic history of ancient Egypt at the École des Hautes Études en Sciences Sociales (EHESS) in Paris. He has published extensively on the administration, socio-economic history, and landscape organization of ancient Egypt, usually in a comparative perspective with other civilizations of the ancient world, and has organized several conferences on these topics.

Anna Stevens
University of Cambridge and Monash University

Anna Stevens is a research archaeologist with a particular interest in how material culture and urban space can shed light on the lives of the non-elite in ancient Egypt. She is Senior Research Associate at the McDonald Institute for Archaeological Research and Assistant Director of the Amarna Project (both University of Cambridge).

About the Series

The aim of this Elements series is to offer authoritative but accessible overviews of foundational and emerging topics in the study of ancient Egypt, along with comparative analyses, translated into a language comprehensible to non-specialists. Its authors will take a step back and connect ancient Egypt to the world around, bringing ancient Egypt to the attention of the broader humanities community and leading Egyptology in new directions.

Cambridge Elements ≡

Ancient Egypt in Context

Elements in the Series

Seeing Perfection: Ancient Egyptian Images Beyond Representation
Rune Nyord

Ethnic Identities in the Land of the Pharaohs: Past and Present Approaches in Egyptology
Uroš Matić

Egypt and the Desert
John Coleman Darnell

Coffin Commerce: How a Funerary Materiality Formed Ancient Egypt
Kathlyn M. Cooney

Ceramic Perspectives on Ancient Egyptian Society
Leslie Anne Warden

The Nile: Mobility and Management
Judith Bunbury and Reim Rowe

The Archaeology of Egyptian Non-Royal Burial Customs in New Kingdom Egypt and Its Empire
Wolfram Grajetzki

Power and Regions in Ancient States: An Egyptian and Mesoamerican Perspective
Gary M. Feinman and Juan Carlos Moreno García

Ancient Egypt in its African Context: Economic Networks, Social and Cultural Interactions
Andrea Manzo

Egyptian Archaeology and the Twenty-First Century Museum
Alice Stevenson

Technology and Culture in Pharaonic Egypt: Actor Network Theory and the Archaeology of Things and People
Martin Fitzenreiter

A full series listing is available at: www.cambridge.org/AECE

Printed in the United States
by Baker & Taylor Publisher Services